Weep No More, Little Project Girl

BETTY SHORT-SAMS

Scripture Identification Scripture quotations marked (AMP) are taken from The Amplified Bible (AMP). The Amplified Bible, Old Testament, copyright © 1965, 1987 by The Zondervan Corporation. The Amplified New Testament, copyright © 1954, 1958, 1987 by The Lockman Foundation. Used by Permission.
Scriptures noted (NIV) are taken from the Holy Bible: New International Version ®. Copyright © 1973, 1978, 1984 by International Bible Society. Used by permission of Zondervan Publishing House. All rights reserved. Scripture quotations marked (NKJV) are taken from the New King James Version. Copyright © 1979, 1980, 1982 by Thomas Nelson, Inc., Publishers. All rights reserved. Scripture quotations marked (NASB) are taken from The New American Standard Bible (NASB). Copyright © 1960, 1962, 1963, 1968, 1971, 1972, 1973, 1975, 1977, 1995 by The Lockman Foundation. Scripture quotations marked (ESV) are taken from The Holy Bible, English Standard Version. ESV ® Text Edition: 2016. Copyright © 2001 by Crossway Bibles, a publishing ministry of Good News Publishers. ISBN 978-1-4555-6022-6 E3-2
For permission requests, email author, addressed "Attention Permissions Coordinator," @ GAPMINISTRIES @ YAHOO.COM

ISBN: 9781096031864

DEDICATION

I dedicate this book to my Quiet Storm, my husband, Clifton. He is a very private man who doesn't believe you need to put your business all out there for all to see or read. I am so thankful to him for allowing me to spread myself naked and unashamed before all who reads this book. I am also appreciative that he never tried to stand in my way when it comes to my God ordained calling. This book is my calling. You are an amazing man, husband, father and Papi. I believe without any doubt that God created you for me, and I am so grateful. I love you with my whole heart. Thank you Cliffy I also dedicate this book to my amazing son, Darnell, and my daughter-in- love Sonia. I am so grateful to God every day for you both and the many blessings that you have added to my life. Thanks to my Grawesome five grandbabies: Lesley, Alicia, Isaiah, Isabella (Bella), and Violet. You are all my precious heartbeats. I hope you know that you have God's Awesome Promises in your life. Dedicate your lives to Him and expect nothing less than greatness from the King! Your continual encouragement and prayers helped me to finish this project. Love you all... Gammie

CONTENTS

	Acknowledgments	i
1	Introduction	1
2	Strategy 1: It's Not Your Fault	6
3	Strategy 2: Ripping Off the Mask	18
4	Strategy 3: Exposing the Predator	34
5	Strategy 4: Who's to Blame	50
6	Strategy 5: Decision or Denial	65
7	Strategy 6: The Celebration	83
8	Conclusion	95

ACKNOWLEDGMENTS

First, I want to thank my Heavenly Father for His continual reminder of His promises for my life. One of His promises was to heal my brokenness. He planted a seed for this book a long, long time ago, but fear kept me from sharing it. I thank God for breaking that chain of fear off of me, and by His grace it is completed. Father I give You all permission to use this project for Your glory and purpose. I like to thank the brave women who shared their stories with me, whom themselves were currently serving time in jail. Thank you for trusting me to tell your story. Thank you for believing in this project and wanting so passionately to be a part of it. Some of you reported receiving healing through sharing their stories. My prayer is that God continues to heal you into complete wholeness. Through the sharing of their stories I pray that there will be healing brought to someone else. I am so grateful to my sister, Linda Joe, who has helped me with the historical recall for this project. There were so many missing pieces that, through God's grace, she was able to give me names and places that I had long forgotten. Joe you are the bravest woman I know. You have overcome so many personal obstacles and you are still going strong. Keep your heart open to receive the many blessings God has for you. I have been so blessed by God to have so many close sisters and friends. Ladies, you know who you are and how special you are to me. There are so many of you who I can count on! I thank you for your prayers, encouragement, and true love that you continue to give me. I would like to thank all of my sisters in Christ at church, my life groups, YAA (You Are Adored-YAA) and women prayer group for their encouragement and prayers as I worked toward finishing this project and work friends . All prayers were heard! I am extremely grateful to my proofreaders. I prayed and asked God to show me who I was to trust with this project and He showed me iv WEEP NO MORE, LITTLE PROJECT GIRL you. So, thank you for saying yes. Thank you for your precious time spent reading and your valuable comments. Special thanks to my God appointed technical advisors, Ms. Dorothy Love. Dorothy thank you for the many hours we shared going over and through this project. And Dolores Haste, thank you for coming along side of me and lifting the big boulders off my shoulders. You recognized I needed help and you called in the calvary Mariam. I appreciated you both more than I can say. All of you were priceless and I will treasure y'all in my heart forever. Last but not least, I got to thank my writing coach, editor and publisher, Felicia Killings of LiyahAmore University, for her coaching style and skills. Felicia, you stayed with me throughout the entire project. You heard and understood my heart in every word written. Your encouragement was priceless, but not free, every dollar spent was well worth it! Thank you for the skills that I learned in writing this project and the projects to come. Bless you, young lady, and many blessings toward your ministries. <u>Without the power of the Holy Spirit and</u> His holy anointing <u>this</u> book would not have been possible. Thank You Lord for every written word. May it be used to go forth and change lives and expose evil!

INTRODUCTION

For so long, I thought less of myself. I was born in Brunswick, Georgia in the mid-1960s to a single mother. There were four kids in all.

As far back as I can remember, we lived in a housing project called Brooklyn Homes. We, of course, were on welfare and were very poor. I pause to laugh about this because I never thought of us as being poor. Afterall, everyone I knew in my world lived just as we did and experienced many of the same experiences I had growing up.

I remember being around several play-cousins. I was one of the youngest of the crew, around five-years-old. My mama would go clubbing with her friends, leaving us with one of the older cousins at my god mama's house, who had a bunch of children of her own.

These were my closest play-cousins. They were my protectors. They guarded me and my sister, Linda, who was two years older than I was.

Linda was mature for her age. She would always think of herself as my mama since our mama worked long hours and on the weekends, she went clubbing whenever she could. And when mama would go out, we would spend the night over to our cousins. These sleepovers were always fun.

It was Linda, Pumpkin, Darryl, and me. Darryl and I were the youngest of the crew. We would play until my god mama Beverly aka Bevie (my god mama and their mama) would yell for us to go to bed. On one of these sleepovers is where I met the first monster in the mask for the first time that I can clearly recall. It is bedtime and everybody jumps into bed, a twin bunk bed and one full size bed was crammed into this little room. We enjoyed going there. My cousin Darryl was on the top bunk, I was too afraid to go up there because I don't like heights, and my sister and cousin Pumpkin was in the lower bunk so that left the full size bed for me and everything was fine we were all asleep until the older cousin came home high on drugs.

He had been drinking too because I could smell the alcohol on his breath. He got into bed with me, it was after all his bed. He got into bed and he took my small little hand and put it on his penis, and he made me rub it and rub it and rub it until it got hard and then wet and then limp.

As I write this, <u>I remember the</u> touch. <u>I remember the</u> horrible <u>feeling of it.</u> I guess now as I sit here and I can say thank you Lord that that was all he did to me but it was still a horrible memory that as I sit here at age 52 I am still remembering it and I am still weeping because it was wrong! It was wrong, and what he did to me was wrong and that it happened to me was wrong! I remember trying to get up and get out of the bed, but he held me down with its other hand until it was over and until he was done. I laid there so scared I just laid there. I heard him snoring and that is when I got up and then I found my sister Linda and I just laid next to her. I was so scared.

The next day I said nothing. I didn't tell a soul. I thought I did something wrong because why would one of my favorite cousins who had protected me, who has never ever done anything like that before, why would he do that to me? I couldn't tell anyone I felt nasty. My hand still had the stickiness on them, and they smelled. I must have done something wrong. I couldn't tell Linda what had happen, since I myself couldn't explain it. I just felt scared and shamed and nasty. But mostly fear is what I felt. Remember y'all I was only 5 years old.

After that experience I grew up scared. Linda used to tell me I was scared of my shadow. Truth be told she was right. I was afraid of what was in the shadows, or should I say who was in them. I lived a life afraid, nervous and lonely. I had people around me, but all the same lonely.

I was molested by different men; they were family members and friends of the family. It happened so often I really thought this was how it was. NORMALCY! Surely, I can't be the only one, or if I am it must be something I'm doing, or there's something wrong with me, right?

WRONG! IT'S NOT MY FAULT! I am going to say this out loud throughout the pages of this book. IT'S NOT YOUR FAULT!

Well I had to surrender my fears to the Lord. I said to the Lord it is not about fame or glamour that I want to write this book, in fact just the opposite because I may well lose some loved ones over this book, but it is not about holding on to those who have been little to absent in my life. It's about stopping another young girl or boy from being attacked by that demonic spirit of molestation. That's what it is all about.

The Lord gave me the idea of this book over 25 years ago. He gave me God's Awesome Promises Ministries in the late 90's. I believe it was when He first was trying to bring healing into my life from the evil abuse of Molestation, but of course I wasn't hearing Him or trusting Him. I didn't really know Him. I knew of Him. I wasn't ready. I'm ready NOW!

I sit here now saying, Lord I can't write this book without your Spirit leading me. I don't know what to say. I don't even know how to say it, but I know it needs to be said! Because this evil is everywhere, and it must be STOP! It has no particular race or sex. It has a name and it effects are long lasting. His/her name is MOLESTATION! Molester, Pervert, Predator, and so many others. It can be familiar in names, father/mother, grandfather/grandmother, uncle/aunt, brother/sister, cousins, and many other names as well as Stranger. It's all the same MURDERER OF THE INNOCENT! MONSTER IN THE MASK! MOLESTER!

So, who am I and why should you want to read anything from me? Well, I am a Nobody that wrote this book for Somebody to let you know that God cares for Everybody. Well, I am you little person, whether you are a youth, teenager, young adult or a grown woman, boy or man, Black, White, Asian, Mexican or whatever, I am you. What do I have to say that would make you turn this page and the next is simple "IT WAS NOT YOUR FAULT"! I remember joining the Sacramento Sheriff Department (SSD) almost 30 years ago. My goal in life was to protect myself and others from harm. My spiritual goal was kind of the same. I wanted to be the first on the scene after the Monster in the Mask, which is what I call the Molester, who had molested a young person so I could look that molested person straight in the eyes and tell them that "THIS WAS NOT YOUR FAULT!"

Now back to who I am, who I really am is still in the process of becoming who I am supposed to be. When I think of myself, I can remember the many years living in torment by not loving myself or others in the right way. I was living in fear of exposure, rejection, guilt and shame. All because of what some other persons had done to me, the Monsters in the Mask. I hated all the wrong people; I was number one on that long list. I gave myself away in many different and difficult ways just to make others feel better about themselves.

<u>I did not know</u> who <u>I was</u> because <u>I</u> myself <u>had</u> been wearing <u>a</u> mask of guilt, shame, low-self-worth, and fear. My mask was so much of a permanent fixture <u>that I didn't know</u> who <u>the</u> real Betty was <u>and</u> what <u>I</u> did know of her I hated!

As you can see the question still hasn't been answered. The question of who am I? Well <u>this is what I</u> can <u>tell you. I am</u> the instrument <u>that</u> God has chosen to use to bring Real Exposure. Needed Exposure! It's time to rip the mask off the Monster and the mask off yourself.

I share these memories because I believe there is someone out there that is still being a victim of the Monsters in the Mask. (From this point on let's call him or her what they are "the Molester").

I believe God will use God's Awesome Promises Ministries to bring restoration to you, young person and bring wholeness to a broken, devastated life. Are you ready to live your life as it was originally created for? Are you ready to S.T.O.P. (Stand, Take, Own & Protect) you and walk in your God given rights and authority as His Daughter? If you can say yes to any of these questions then I can positively say YOU are ready to L.I.V.E. (Love, Invest in, Value & Enjoy) your life!

<u>As you read this book</u> know <u>that you</u> can ask <u>God</u> for His help in breaking the holds of …whatever… is on or in your life, whether its fear, shame, guilt, a lustful spirit (I will explain this one

later in the book), hate, or unforgiveness, because of what happened to you or is happening to you. Let God use this little project girl's story to bring healing and wholeness into a dead and barren land called your life. He did it for me!

STRATEGY 1: IT'S NOT YOUR FAULT

I remember the moment I decided to become a deputy sheriff. My number one reason was I wanted to be the first one on the scene to tell a young girl who had been assaulted that it wasn't her fault. How I wish I had someone to tell me this when I was a little girl. Oh, how freeing it would have been to know that I was not the one with the problem, but they were.

Quite often, when women are molested, their first thoughts center on "It's my fault." There is this lack of understanding of why it's happening. It also has to do with why this person is doing this to me. Is this wrong? Am I guilty for not saying something? Is it something I wanted? Is it wrong that I like this feeling? Is it really wrong?

The answer is yes, it is wrong, but it's not your fault.

In this chapter, I will share with you my personal story of being molested and raped by family members and a friend of the family. And then I will share with you the story of a young lady that is currently incarcerated (Let's call her Shae Shae) Shae Shae and how her sexual abuse led to her incarceration.

MY STORY

I remember the many times my sister Linda and I would go to our Big Mama Laura and Big Daddy Crook's house in Cordelia, Georgia. My mama would send us to them every summer. My brother Philip, he was the oldest and my sister Michelle lived there with them. These visits gave us the opportunity to spend time with them since this is the only time of the year, we would get to see them. My brother Philip was six years older than me and I remember him as being a quiet dark-skinned boy.

My sister, Michelle, was five years older than me. She was very pretty to me. She was a mixed race (half-breed) is what we called her. She was high yellow (light skinned) with thick wavy black hair. It was an exciting time getting to see them until we got there.

Michelle was very mean to me. She was what you would call "evil- spirited" and hot tempered. I never understood why she hated me, but I understand now. Knowing what I know now, I can't imagine having to live with such a horrible man as Otis "Crook" Reddings. Having been molested by him every time we went there, what on earth did she have to endure living there with that monster every day? Only God knows.

Years later I asked her on several occasions if he had ever done anything to her and she would get angry and strongly deny it ever happened. She didn't believe it happened to me either. She always defended him every time I would tell her he did molest me.

These conversations came up when I would ask her why she became an addict. Anyone who knew my sister knew of her battle with that demon of addiction. This is not me speaking ill of the dead. I loved my sister until the day God called her home to Him. I asked her if she used drugs because she was trying to forget things from her past. She said she just got caught up using. It's not for me to tell her story, but I can tell you that I have had the opportunity to talk with so many other women whose life was similar to my sister, and they all told me that their usage started out small and went downhill quickly. One of them told me that her reason for using was to get the bad man out of her head. Another one wanted the voices to stop assaulting her by telling her she was nothing and was no good. They wanted to stop the painful memories from coming in their minds, so they silenced the pain by using drugs.

The Holy Spirit brought to my memory all the years of being a deputy assigned to the women detention facility; I told them that the abuse was not their fault. The abuse led to their crime, but the abuse was not their fault. My reason for being open with them was in hope of stopping the cycle of young girls being abused and having them end up in jail years later because they didn't understand that they have choices. It's not about what people did to them or decided for them. It's about them making the right choices and the right-now choices for their lives. There's a different way, a greater way. And this led me to asking the women to share their stories with me.

SHAE SHAE'S STORY

I was five years old when my innocence got taken. This is how I got turned onto prostitution. My Cousin Vicki's husband, Tony, would come into my room at night when he got off of work. He would come in while I was asleep. The first time he molested me that I can remember was when he came in and started rubbing on my breast and then moved on from not just rubbing my breast but now sucking on them. He moved on to playing with my private parts and started rubbing it with his penis. He quickly moved from playing with my private to putting his penis inside of it. When he started putting his penis in me, he started giving me money every time. He would put the money under my pillow. A couple of days before I turned six years old, he came in my room and laid down next to me. He played with my breast then moved down to my privates and this night he put his mouth on me and started to proceed with oral sex, and then he put his penis inside of me and started moving up and down until he ejaculated. He laid there for a minute and then gave me some money. The next morning when I woke up, I had on my Tweety Bird pajamas there was blood all over my pajama pants. I told his wife, my cousin, about the blood in my pj's she said I just started my period.

The molesting went on another time when Vicki went on a vacation with her sisters like always and Tony and his niece Brandy was babysitting us and Brandy was trying to lay me down for a nap. I was laying <u>in the middle of</u> her <u>and</u> Tony. <u>I didn't</u> want to take a nap, so she <u>gave me something to drink. I</u> thought it <u>was</u> some orange juice, so I drunk it. Well that was <u>all I</u> remember. <u>I don't know</u> exactly <u>what</u> she gave me <u>or</u> what they did to me, but I know I was molested. As I grew older it was a regular thing for Tony to come into my room and do whatever he wanted to me. The only thing he hadn't done to me yet was sodomize me. The older I got the more money he would leave me. I kept the money hid until one day Vicki was going shopping at Walmart and she took me with her. I bought a new Bratz phone. I realized it was real when I got home, plugged it in and dialed the house phone. Vicki answered the phone, so I hung it up. She found I had the phone, so she thought I stole it from Walmart. She beat the daylights out of me. She kicked me all in my stomach and blackened my eyes. She pulled my hair out and then she took the phone back to Walmart. Vicki had a lot of anger *toward me, so much so that she didn't stop beating me until she saw blood or got tired. After the beatings, Tony would always come in my room to "console" me or should I say console himself. I found out from Brandy that all of Tony's sisters (including her own mom) were molested by Tony's dad. Tony and his brothers were also molesters. Brandy told me that all the nieces (including herself) were molested by one of them.*

When I was 13 years old, I finally told Vicki what had been going on because I found out that Tony was touching on my little sister. She was only seven years old. I caught him in the act of that assault. I told him if he didn't leave her alone, I would tell Vicki. I told her anyway because I didn't believe him when he said he wouldn't touch her. Well I told Vicki and she confronted him. My sister and I heard him admit to touching on me. He didn't care what she thought. Her response shocked me. She said, "Well I don't give a f--- as long as you don't touch on the little ones."

That next day I decided to run away from her house. I was hanging out at a friend of mine house until the next day. My friend told me I couldn't stay at her house because she had to go to her grandmother's funeral the next day. So, I had nowhere else to go so my friend called Vicki and told her where I was and asked for her to come and get me. Vicki and my older brother Antoine came and picked me up. Antoine kept smiling and laughing at me when I got in the car. I didn't think much of it until we stopped at the Children's Receiving Home. Vicki told me to get out of the car. I thought it was a daycare or counseling center. She told them she was coming back so I thought that meant she was coming back for me. Well she did come back and with her was all my clothes and stuffed animals. <u>That was the last time I saw my</u> little sister, and both of my brothers, eventually they all moved to Texas.

I am now twenty-three years old. Tony still tries to this day to get in touch with me through Facebook. This might sound weird but after a while I started to miss his touch. This is very sickening. I can't find love or that right pleasure unless it is with him. I sent him pictures of my private part and my breast. He still gives me money. He would send me messages telling me he misses my lips, body, and touch. <u>It's</u> like <u>I don't know how</u> to shake him.

I feel like my life would have been better if I just kept my mouth shut and not have told Vicki what Tony was doing, I would be successful like my little sister is and living a very wonderful life. Every time I get into a new relationship it never last for more than a year. If they try to touch me in the night, it's all bad. Tony and Vicki really messed up my life mentally, emotionally, and physically. I have nightmares about me falling in love with Tony and we have kids together. I would even have dreams of us making love and it will either cause me to wake up out of a dead sleep or sometimes I would be turned on. I would wake up feeling bad about myself because those dreams and thoughts are not right.

No one has ever told Shae Shae that what happened to her was not her fault.

In Shae's story, she is still living her hell because she hasn't found the key to her prison gate yet. She is still locked in victim mode. She still feels her abusers owe her something for what they did to her. But there isn't any amount of money or apology that will fix or repay what has been stolen. I pray that Shae Shae finds the key that will unlock her from the past so that she can S.T.O.P. her future self. I pray her pain and sadness will turn into total healing from the past.

BIG DADDY

I was talking to Linda the other day out of the blue about how and where we were raised. I was telling her about Big Daddy (he was our mom's uncle) and what he did to me when we use to go to Cordelia Georgia for the summer. He labored as a freemason, building churches, of all things, and would take me on worksites with him. Well during these visits, he would tell me to get in the backseat of his car and rape me, full blown penetration. Let's not call it having sex, because that would imply consent. I was a child that learned quickly that if I gave into it (the sexual act) then I would get a treat (bribe/reward) afterwards.

Those treats ranged from food, money, or just being his favorite (so I thought), which means I got away with not getting my butt whipped. He would come in and "protect" me, not realizing that he was the one I needed protecting from. Well these kinds of things happened all the time when we were there.

As I was sharing this story, my sister began to get emotional and cry. She shared with me that she would let that same uncle do it to her so that he wouldn't do it to me. She thought that sacrificing herself was going to stop him from coming after me. This is what she has always done for people, even those who did not deserve her self- sacrificing.

MR. JOHN

Mr. John Richards was my most horrific predator! He was a Jamaican and a friend of my mom's boyfriend, Junior. He <u>was a member of</u> our church, <u>First</u> African <u>Baptist Church of</u> Brunswick. <u>He</u> song in the choir. He had a beautiful tenor voice. He and his wife, Ms. Thelma, became my "godparents", which was strange because I already had a god mama that I loved. Ms. Thelma couldn't have kids of her own, so that is why I figure she became my god mama. I was about eight or nine years old when he started coming around regularly. Mama's friend, Junior, was gone, nowhere to be found, so this is why I thought Mr. John was coming around to see mama. He was really friendly with everyone, generous with his money and time. I would see him giving mama money, which was not strange because boyfriends give girlfriends money all the time, right? So that was why when he started his abusing me sexually and I said <u>I didn't want to,</u> he told me <u>that I had to</u> because he gave my mama money so he can have me; and <u>if I didn't do it</u> mama was going to get in trouble and go to jail, and he would leave and I would be alone. This frightened me terribly. I didn't want mama in jail, <u>and I didn't want him to</u> leave me. <u>I</u> was always around him when he was there.

Years later I found pictures of me sitting in his lap in the front yard. He took a great liking to me. He would make me feel special. I was happy when he was there. All was good until it wasn't. He would take me to get food and we would bring it back for us all to eat. This happened all the time. I guess that is why it wasn't strange for mama to let me go with him whenever he would come by. I mentioned earlier that he and Ms. Thelma were my godparents but come to think of it, I never once can remember Ms. Thelma coming to the projects where we lived. I would see her on occasions at her home, but never at mama's. (Maybe that is why I thought mama and Mr. John was seeing each other.)

Mr. John and Ms. Thelma had a beautiful three- or four-bedroom, one-story home in what us project people call the "white" neighborhood. It was on a corner lot with a big yard. I couldn't believe black people really lived like this, although some of the kids who lived in this neighborhood did go to school with me. Of course, they didn't hang out or played with me. We never travelled out to the Magnolia Park area. We had no reason to. Nothing out there we needed.

I can't remember exactly when the first actual act of molestation happened, but I do know that the abuse happened at his house. I had been to his house on several occasions. One of my memories were of his taking me into one of the bedrooms and having sex with me. I had to be about ten years old. I was <u>in so much pain that I</u> bled. I <u>can't</u> remember if this was the first penetration act with him. He sat on the floor next to the bed where I was lying, and he rubbed my back as I hurt. He told me that it will be alright, and the pain was going to stop the more we do it.

He was upset about the blood on the sheets. He had to wash them before Ms. Thelma came home. There are so many more vulgar acts of molestation/rape committed against me. One thing I wanted to share is that what the enemy (Satan) meant for evil in my life, his plans for taking me out of the game , turned out to be used for my good. You may ask how, well the answer is simple and yet powerful. I could have remained in victim mode and allowed the molesters of this world continue to write my story or stand against the lies, fear, and shame by telling my story to you in hopes that it will help you through your healing process.

Ironically, being exposed to John's world gave me a glimpse of <u>what I could have. I didn't</u> want <u>to</u> live in the projects or be raised on welfare. I wanted to go to college, and I did not want to have a lot of kids from different men, just to become another single mother on welfare. I wanted to be married to my kids' father. Even though the molestation was horrible, I still found a way to see how I could grow from it.

Ms. Thelma, when she was not working, would have her two nieces over and we would all play. This didn't happen too often because Ms. Thelma worked for the postal service, so she was always working. Whenever the nieces were over, we would have to play hide and seek. Mr. John was always the one who did the seeking. He would tell us we would have to hide by ourselves, and when we did this, I would remember him touching my chest and putting his hand down my panties and putting his fingers up me; then he would go on to the next hider. When we didn't hide separately, he would get so mad and stop the game. The three of us would just go outside and play.

I noticed the girls stopped coming after a while. I just thought since Ms. Thelma was always working, they couldn't visit.

I didn't think much about it until years later. They must have told Ms. Thelma what Mr. John did to them, and that was why she finally divorced him. At least someone came to their rescue, right.

After the divorce she moved in with her sister and then moved out of town. I don't know where. She never kept in touch with me, after all we didn't really have a godmother-to-daughter relationship. I always wondered if she knew. Well that question was answered years later when she came back to Brunswick to visit with her family. I was about sixteen years old. She called mama and asked for me. She told mama she wanted to see me while she was in town. So, she gave mama her sister's phone number and address. I went and visited.

During the visit she was strangely quiet, not distant just quiet. She told me she wanted to see how I was doing and that she wanted to tell me she was sorry. This, I didn't understand, because she had never done anything to me. I didn't understand that by saying or doing nothing, she was a part of the assault. Of course, this understanding came many years later. I never hated Ms. Thelma since I always felt sorry for her. She was an obese woman, very overweight. She had a beautiful face, but a sad one. I remember times when she would get home and I was there she would tear up. There were times when Mr. John was so mean to her. He would yell at her, push on her, and call her horrible names. This would make her cry. I didn't understand why she put up with it. I remember when she transitioned from the obese Thelma to the slimmer, more put together Thelma. She joined Weight Watchers and started working out and losing weight like crazy. John became more openly abusive toward her in front of me. Thinking about it now, he was scared because she was getting ready to toss his butt to the curb. The truth of the matter is she was his paycheck, his dinner ticket. She worked consistently. He was a painter and worked as the jobs came.

John's abuse became not just sexual but physical as I got older. I was around twelve or thirteen at this time, having my periods and starting to develop physically. He would come over and try to get me to go with him and I would say no because I wasn't feeling well. He would grab me by my arms and squeeze them until I teared up. He did not care if I was on my period or not. He just wanted complete control of me.

I finally told my neighbor Mattie Mae. She was a young wife and mother of two boys. She was so beautiful. Her apartment was next to ours. I was always hanging out over there when her husband wasn't home. She was a lonely woman. So, I spent time there until I felt safe enough to share with her. When I told her what John was doing to me, I made her promise not to tell mama, since I <u>didn't want to get into</u> any trouble. <u>So,</u> she and <u>I</u> had an agreement if John came over I was to come to her house through the back door. I could hide in her downstairs closet until he left. He would hang around for a while because mama use to tell him I was just there she <u>didn't know where I went, but I</u> should be back soon. So, he would wait. Mattie Mae and I watched him from her front window until he would be visibly mad and then he would get in his car and leave. This happened a number of times. I laugh about it now, but on several occasions he would come back that same day, demanding to know where I was, but these times I couldn't hide because her husband would be home so I would have to face him.

Mattie Mae was a timely sent angel for me. She died very young from cancer. I was in the military living overseas when I found out in a letter from mama. My heart ached for this lady's passing, but I know she is with the Lord because, like I said, she was one of His angels sent from above.

When I was twelve, I went to a church service with one of my aunts. During this service, I remember the preacher asking if anyone wanted to ask Jesus into their life and be saved. Of course, not really understanding what that meant, he continued saying, "If there is anything you need to be saved from, come and get Jesus and He will save you from all your troubles." I remember getting up and going to the altar, asking Jesus in my life. <u>I don't even remember</u> walking up <u>there I was</u> just there. I wanted Jesus, because to my understanding, at that age was that He was going to come and stop all the sexual and physical abuse I was going through.

Well it didn't, and it continued for another three years with John. I don't want anyone to think that accepting Jesus into my life was like "Yippee! All is right with the world. I will have no more problems, hurts, abuse and pain because now I am saved." Well, truth be told, the trajectory (direction) of my life changed somewhat, but as that girl who wanted so much for this to be my answer, I didn't recognize it at all. I was unhappy and depressed, sick with ulcers and many other medical conditions.

What I didn't realize was that I saw myself in a love relationship with John. When he was nice, he was generous and when he was angry, he was mean and cold. All I wanted was to be loved. I didn't have a good example of a man in my life; I had real father issues or lack thereof. When I realized that John was not mama's boyfriend but mine, I felt like I owed him. I was trapped in what I thought was a normal relationship. Everything was a give and take. Nothing was for free. Everything was abuse.

I can't remember exactly when the abuse started, but I know I finally started saying no to it when I was 13 or 14 years old. I would fight with him, giving him big attitude just to get him mad at me and he would leave. He would, however, get back at me by not coming around to see me; or if he did come around, he talked to everyone but me. He was extremely manipulative. This made me sad and lonely.

Later, he had fallen on hard times, living in a boarding house renting a room, so he hung around our house, and watching me and trying to control where I was going and with whom. About this time mama had been seeing Mr. Tip. He was an awesome man to me! He was the first man I have ever met that didn't take anything from me. He was the first man I loved as a father. I believe he was the one that started asking mama why John was always around us and why I was always leaving with him. She really didn't think much of it. He had turned into this uncle type person to her, so I guess that was her thoughts.

Well mama hadn't said anything to me until one night when I was taking a bath and she came into the bathroom, close the door behind her, and stood over the tub. Now I got to give you a visible picture of my mama. She was about 5'10, 190 to 220 lbs. on a light day. She was big and dark skinned. She chewed tobacco and pretty much kicked the butts of most of her boyfriends. She was a real, bad country woman. Now with that said, she stood over me and asked me with piercing, dark brown eyes, if John had ever messed with me or touched me in a wrong way. Even then no one used the word molest or rape. (Remember I didn't know it had a name.) Well I was quick to answer her because I didn't want to get into trouble. So, I quickly said, "No! He never did anything to me." She stared at me for a second. When she closed the door, I <u>cried and</u> cried. <u>I was terrified. I don't know</u> why <u>I</u> defended him except for the fact that I believed I was doing something wrong, too.

Over time, my life became busier. I was in high school with friends that I enjoyed being with. John wasn't as clingy around this time. The sex only happened when I wanted to get money from him. I knew it was over with him when I turned fifteen. I went to his boarding house one day to get some money from him. Of course, I knew what that meant. If I wanted money, I had to give up sex. Well when I got there, two little girls ran out from the house. <u>I didn't know if</u> they lived there <u>or not but</u> they came out laughing with each other. They looked as if they were seven or eight years of age. I knocked on his door and then opened it. He was putting a shirt on, so I went in and asked him for money. He told me no. He said he was tired of my coming around just to get money from him. He said he didn't want me coming over any more. I was actually hurt by this because I thought I was in control of this relationship. I went by there a couple more times to see if he was serious. I saw him on the front porch once being really friendly with some little girls that were sitting on the porch with him. Well he was serious. He had actually moved on to younger girls. I remember seeing how friendly he was with the little girls on his porch. It was the same friendliness that I had received years earlier. Years later I realized that this was my first experience of rejection.

You know while writing this I asked God a question: when did the abuse really stop? And why didn't I stop earlier? At age fifteen, was I making it a choice to continue with him? WRONG! Let me be honest with you: I thought I was in a normal relationship. But it wasn't normal, and no girl should ever experience this. Eventually, I had to realize that the assault wasn't my fault, and in order for me to overcome my internal sickness and pain, I had to do something about it. This is the lesson I want to teach you to do so you can conquer this monster.

1. **Tell your story.** Sometimes the best way to tell your story is to share it in writing for yourself. Releasing the memories of what happened to you can help you get through the trauma, by seeing it and releasing it.

2. **Remind yourself OFTEN that it was not your fault.** Maybe it doesn't feel like it right now, but you must remember that what happened to you at any age wasn't your fault.
3. **Take comfort in knowing that you can overcome this.** I wrote this book because there are proven strategies that I have used to help me. This book also contains references from other sources that will help you along the way.

STRATEGY 2: RIPPING OFF THE MASK

Mask: A covering for all or part of the face, worn as a disguise, or to amuse or terrify other people. A disguise, <u>false face.</u> <u>A covering worn on the face to conceal one's identity.</u>

When I think about the different people who wear masks throughout their lives and why they wear them, this makes me think about my own reason. For so many years I wanted people to think of me as a well put together lady. A woman who was a good wife, mother, Christian, cop and friend. If only they knew my truth. I wanted to be all those things, but I failed to see what was good in me that could come out if they knew what I really looked like. Not my outer face but my inner self. You know a well put together person on the outside but a shattered figure on the inside. No one knew my fears, shame and guilt. No one, not even my husband. Thinking of the masks I wore, (different ones for different people) this made me think of this poem "We Wear the Mask" by Paul Laurence Dunbar

We wear the Mask that grins and lies,
It hides our cheeks and shades our eyes, This debt we pay to human guile;
With torn and bleeding hearts we smile, And mouth with myriad subtleties.
Why should the world be over-wise, In counting all our tears and sighs?
Nay, let them see us, while We Wear the Mask.

> *We smile, but, O great Christ, our cries To thee from tortured souls arise.*
> *We sing, but oh the clay is vile Beneath our feet, and long the mile;*
> *But let the world dream otherwise, We Wear the Mask! [1]*

What is <u>the mask</u> symbolic of in <u>Paul Laurence Dunbar'</u>s poem? The mask <u>refers to people hiding their true feelings behind a false expression. Specifically, he is referring to the cheerful face that so many blacks felt necessary to wear in front of</u> their oppressors. <u>Dunbar was an African American poet, and he is speaking about the facade that many blacks wear (wore) to hide their inner pain and suffering from the world. The mask that is worn is a happy face that hides the tears and the tear-stained cheeks as well as the sad and hurting heart. In the second stanza, the speaker declares that the mask keeps the world from seeing the sorrows of the African Americans, and questions why the world should be privy to this pain. The smiles and song only cover the pain of the "tortured soul: and mask the cries that arise from the sorrow. The world is content with the illusion of the African American happiness, and the speaker of the poem sees no reason to disabuse</u> (set straight) the world of its misconception. He and his fellow African Americans will continue to wear the mask. [2]

This poem does speak so strongly to me, simply because the mask is something we wear today, not because of slavery and racial injustice. But because of the prisons of oppression, pain, shame, guilt and fear that we see every time we look at ourselves through the eyes of others. Our perception of what others think of us is so powerful. We would rather wear a lie than step out in front of the lie and scream, "IT'S ME, HERE I AM AND THIS IS ALL I HAVE TO GIVE. TAKE IT OR LEAVE IT!"

What stopped me from taking my mask off was simply FEAR. I didn't like the girl/woman behind the mask, so how would anyone else? I saw myself through my abuse. I didn't realize it because it was normal for me to hide and perform to everyone's liking. A real people pleaser! Or at least I try to please others. It was good to learn that you will never be able to please some or all the people EVER! They are forever changing on you.

This is where I relate to the poem above. When it <u>points specifically to the hardships and suffering of slaves</u> (prisoners). <u>They were placed in such harsh conditions</u> (rape/trafficked), <u>and yet</u>

they did not show the pain (on the outside). They did not wear their emotions on their sleeves. They made every effort to appear happy and content, while underneath the facade, they were emotionally torn up and beaten down. [3]

What do you do when you are emotionally torn? Some run away to escape only to find themselves in an even worse condition. Others like Christina who shared Her Story with me. Christina explains why she wanted to share so please give attention to her story below.

CHRISTINA in her own words

>*I come from an Asian family; I was raised by a single mother of five. Growing up wasn't a pleasant experience for me. All of my innocence stopped at the age of nine. I have two older sisters and two younger brothers, and me being the middle child. My sisters were never really close as I am to my little brothers. My mother did all she could to raise all of her children. She also was in different relationships with men who would abuse her. I never understood why she attracted those type of men. All I knew was when she cried, I cried. When I was 9, she was involved with a man who she became pregnant with. This same man ended up raping me and molesting me until I was 12. I was broken inside and out. My spirit was driven to the ground. What was once a happy and vivacious child was now filled with self-hatred; and my innocence robbed. No matter how many people told me how beautiful I was and would become, inside I felt so ugly, unworthy, and violated. In school I struggled with my school assignments. My grades went from straight "A" student to becoming a "D-"student. People started noticing the drastic changes in my behavior. Inside I would scream for help, hoping someone would hear my cries. But I also tried to wear a MASK to hide the hurt I was going through. The man also threatened to kill me and my mother if I ever said anything to anyone about what he was doing to me. Like a scared innocent child would, I kept silent.*
>
>*Until one night, December 16, 1996, I ran away from home to escape the nightmare I was living. It was my middle school's winter ball. That night I built up the courage to leave. Two weeks of disappearing from home, someone who knew my mother called her to tell her that they knew my whereabouts. She arrived at the home I had been hiding at which was a friend of mine from school. My mother finally discovered what was happening to me. The man she was with beat her almost half to death. Threatening if she told the authorities anything he would definitely kill her. My mother arranged for me to live with my father who lives in San Jose, Ca. She advised me to never tell my father what transpired in her home. In fear of someone getting killed behind the situation, so again, I kept silent.*

Two weeks into being in this new city and I had already enrolled into a different school, made new friends, and explored the amazing tow. I thought life was back to normal and how a kid should live. One night my uncle (my father's brother), came into my room while I was asleep. He climbed in my bed and violated (raped) me just like my mother's boyfriend had. My world was then shattered once more. At that point I believed <u>that I couldn't trust</u> no one. <u>I felt</u> so <u>confused</u> as to why <u>I</u> was a target. I ended up running away from my father's house. I was a teenage kid fending to care for myself with no guidance, no street smarts...NOTHING!

My dreams of growing up was to become a beautician and a computer engineer. Something my father wanted for me and what I was good at doing at a young age. Was I capable of still reaching my goals and dreams? My ambition and determination had died.

I had stayed at random people's houses. Some I would've just met and, of course were a little older than <u>I was.</u> So <u>I had to</u> lie about <u>my</u> age <u>so that I</u> would be accepted into the circle of adult life (ANOTHER MASK). If people found out the truth about my age, I knew for sure I would have been reported and would have to go back to the nightmare waiting for me at home.

The group of friends I associated myself with introduced me to the lifestyle of drugs, gangs, and money. I nurtured that lifestyle for so long it became a learned behavior and who I am today. It got me nowhere at age seventeen. I had a child, a son. Today, I am thirty-five and the streets have robbed me of the relations I am to have with my son as a mother. I've struggled to better myself time and again. But because of my loyalty to the streets, my attempt to do better and to have a better life never reached its goal.

I know one thing, I never gave up. I kept my faith in God, the only One who carried me through it all. All the abuse from the men and family members, physically, mentally, sexually, and emotionally. God saw me through it. My passion now is to help adolescents and children who are going through the same things I went through. I had attended college courses for child psychology and early childhood development to become a mentor and therapist. I want to be a support system to kids who lack in that area. To give them the assurance that they are worth loving and that life has a lot to offer.

For those who are reading this don't lose hope, keep reaching for your goals. If you are being violated, I encourage you to tell the authorities, a teacher, or someone you trust. Don't be scared, God will protect you. God bless you.

Here's a Word from the Bible that I pray will give you strength. It gives me strength every day and I know I am not alone. <u>Ecclesiastes 4:9-12 (NIV)</u>

Two are better than one,
  because they have a good return for their labor:
If either of them falls down,
  one can help the other up.
But pity anyone who falls
  and has no one to help them up.
Also, if two lie down together, they will keep warm.
  But how can one keep warm alone?
Though one may be overpowered,
  two can defend themselves.
A cord of three strands is not quickly broken.

If you have a problem depending on men or people in general, like I did, you are not alone, but there is One who you can learn to trust in and be loved by and His name is Jesus Christ. I promise you, He will never leave you nor forsake you. He will be your best friend if you let Him in. He is able to heal and redeem you from all brokenness. He is your hope for a future that is free from all bondages. So, call on Him now! I did! Christina, like so many others, lived a life of escaping from the abuse. She ran away only to find herself in even more danger and grief. But through all her bad she found good. She found it in being a mom to a son who she so adores. She found it in a relationship with the Lover of her soul, Jesus Christ.

I asked Jesus Christ into my life at age 12. Not knowing what that fully meant, I thought I lost Him since nothing had changed in my life really. The abuse was still going on and I was still fearful of being exposed. My Mask was fitted for me at such an early age. I held onto it for so long, from childhood all the way into adulthood. I asked God so many times to heal me from my guilt and shame of the sexual promiscuity and of course the pains that resulted from my molesters; and the healing never came, so I thought. I realized that I was asking for healing but wasn't ready to completely let go of my fears, therefore I was unable to receive His healing. It was like if I did let go of it the shame would come out!

Sex became my enemy as well as my weapon. I <u>didn't want</u> to have <u>sex, in fact, I hated sex.</u> I hated being touch! I didn't even want anyone to see me naked. I was so broken from my abuse, so I had to put on a Mask of a "sex-fiend." I wanted to be loved, liked, accepted and appreciated so the other Mask of "pleasing people" would come on. Growing up in high school I knew coming from the projects and living on welfare made me less than the other folks that I knew. I wanted to be liked by them and be accepted as their friend. Some of them lived in homes with both moms and dads. They lived in the white neighborhoods. These neighborhoods were anywhere off Altama Ave, past Jane Macon Middle School. This is what I thought as a girl who lived her whole childhood, preteen, and teenage years in the housing projects. We went from Brooklyn Homes Projects to Albert Andrews Terrace Projects. We went from a three-bedroom two story unit to a five-bedroom one story unit. Yeah, we thought we had moved up into the big times. Well it really was better living for us at the time. But when measuring myself to everyone else I still wasn't good enough. Mind you, no one ever said these things to me. It was what I repeated to myself constantly.

Going through high school I felt I had to belong to something greater than me. I needed structure and guidance. I wanted to identify with something that would make me stand out. This something to me at the time was Navy Junior Recruit Officer Training Corp (NJROTC). I joined it in the tenth grade. I met some solid friends, who to this day I can still say that I am friends with. One recently went to be with the Lord, but a few others are still around. This type of structured training opened my thinking. It also gave me an identity. I could really see myself in the military, especially when I was dressed out in uniform. I could see options for my life. I still thought I was going to college, but when that didn't happen, I had military to go into. Options, exposure, and decisions were all in my control. No matter what was happening to me or had happened to me, at the end of the day it was still my decision on what <u>the rest of my life</u> was going <u>to</u> look like.

I had to make the final decision as a teenager what Mask I was or was not going to wear. <u>At that time in my life</u>

<u>I was</u> wearing so many. I found myself living in a new mask. This one was called "the church girl mask." This mask made me feel guilty all the time. Since I asked Christ in my life, I should try to live like I belong with Him right? Well that old devil was there too. Again, I wanted to be accepted, so I continued to be a people pleaser. Where on earth is it written in the Bible to please people? Nowhere! But we still put on that mask every Sunday and perform to the best of our abilities, which is always not enough.

I have talked to people who were raised in the church and their parents were in leadership. They were required to be active in most of the ministries and had to wear the mask of perfection. You know you got to make everyone think your household and parents are perfect, no matter what the truth is. Some of these same people told me that once they got to a certain age they immediately rebelled against their parents and church, and they walked away from God. They saw the human weaknesses in the church, and they equated it with Jesus Christ. I did the same thing.

My first memory of playing church was when I was sent to church on the Pentecost bus <u>when I was a little girl.</u> The only thing <u>I</u> knew of Jesus <u>was</u> that He was white with long hair. The leaders gave us red Kool-Aid and cookies and took us back home. Years later and many dress performances for Easter and Christmas Sunday, I joined the youth choir. I found great disappointment in the church because the Masks were still on and I found myself still needing to be accepted by these people who only took advantage of me. I gave myself to them sexually and mentally.

I fell in love with the assistant choir leaders. I thought I was going to marry this guy. Mind you I was still in high school. He said he loved me, and I believed him. He <u>was going to be</u> a pastor <u>and I was going to</u> be a pastor's wife, another mask. I freely gave myself to him sexually so that this dream would come true.

His sister was, who I thought, my best friend. We hung out all the time. I thought she had my back. Her brother broke my heart by breaking up with me telling me he needed time alone and some space to figure out his future. Well what

I found out was my best friend (his sister) set him up with another girl who had just joined our choir. He was now seeing her while we all were still in the choir. How devastated I was to be hurt by them both. I felt so betrayed. What was sad about this was my so-called friend did not deny it when I asked her? I can't remember why she said she did it, but she did not have any regrets for doing it. What was even sadder is I remained friends (or so-called friends) with her because I did not want to be rejected by her, her family and our church friends. Oh, but how painful it was to see him and the girl hanging out with each other. How stupid I felt when I saw the pity in the eyes of some of the other choir members. My point of this story is that bad things don't happen just at home, school, and at work but even at church and, if it can happen at church, it can happen anywhere. I want you to understand that people, places, and things do not make you a better or a grander person. Your true worth does not come through the things of this world. I have lived many years and have learned that true worth only comes through knowing yourself and seeing yourself through the eyes of Christ Jesus, not this world and not the people.

Just this year, three famous, rich and successful people took their own life. This proves that life, family, and riches are many times not enough, and knowing special people or traveling to famous places, nor owning things make you a better. So many people wear a Mask to hide their struggle with depression, anxiety, and addiction. These struggles are huge with our young people. Suicide is at an all-time high in teens, both girls and boys, ages 15 to 19. There are also growing concerns in the ages of 10 to 14 years old as well. <u>Experts say there are multiple reasons more young people are struggling with their mental health. Heavy social media use, bullying, economic burdens, family issues and exposure to violence</u> [4] are among them. Some are victims of abuse, be it sexual, physical, emotional, or mental abuse. This can lead to risk factors for conditions like depression, anxieties and addictive behaviors.

The struggle does not have to be yours to live. I can see now that my having made the best decision of my life at age 12 paved this road of life for me. Again, the trajectory of my existence changed. Now I can clearly see how the Lord's hand was on my life and He is with me all the days of my life. At age 11 and 13, I attempted suicide by taking my mom's pills. Obviously I was not successful in my attempt at committing suicide praise God, but I can relate to the reasoning for wanting to end it all. The hopelessness in such an act is a debilitating state to be in. With great joy I can say I am no longer hopeless, unloved, good for nothing and purposeless.

As I aged, I got TIRED of wearing the Masks of lies that I had received from others. I started learning new thoughts and believing better for and about myself by renewing my mind, washing it with the Word of God, which says I am LOVED, PRECIOUS, AND WANTED!

Here's my charge to you: Take off the MASK! Rip it off, layer by layer. Make the decision that will give you a new life, a life more abundantly. Make a change for the better. Choose your future, letting go of the hurt, pain and shame, and release the past to the past. Reach for a life worth living and forgive.

The decision was finally made for me when I said yes to write this book. I knew the Mask of shame, guilt, and pain was going away as I emptied my story on every page. I trust that through your experience of sharing your story it would help you find true freedom.

Make the decision right now to believe God more than believing your feelings, what you want, or what you think. Make the right decision right now and believe! <u>Make a commitment right now to spend the rest of your life learning how to enjoy the best life God has to</u> offer you through Christ.

Ephesians 2:10 talks about life when it says:

"For we are God's (own) handiwork (His workmanship) recreated in Christ Jesus, (born anew) that we may do these good works which God predestined (planned beforehand) for us (taking paths which He prepared ahead of time), that we should walk in them (living the good life which He prearranged and made ready for us to live)."

Take a moment and go back and slowly read the Scripture that was just quoted; really think about what it is saying to you. Here it is paraphrased by an amazing author who I cherish as one who helped me know Christ through her teaching, and writings: [2] Ephesians 2:10 paraphrased: God created us; we are His workmanship. Because of sin we live broken lives, but through the salvation offend in Jesus we are born again, or made new once again. We get to start over and learn how to do things right. God has always had a good plan for His people and He always will. It is available to anyone who will choose it and learn how to walk in it.

This is what ripping off the Mask looked like for me:

1. Making the decision that I no longer wanted to wear the mask anymore. Believing that this was not who God created me to be. The enemy can't have my future just because he tried to take out my youth.
2. Deciding to believe in myself as a good person, not a waste of life. What God create is good. God does not make junk!
3. Letting go of being controlled by the words and actions of others. I'm not ugly, stupid, poor, or worthless. I have value and worth. I give value to others.

Once the decision has been made to Rip off your Masks ask yourself the following questions:

What does it look like to remove my Mask?
1) _____
2) _____
3) _____

How do I know if the Masks are gone?
1) _____
2) _____
3) _____

What are my most hopeful aspirations for my life?
1) _____
2) _____
3) _____

What does healing, or being made whole, look like for me?

1) _____
2) _____
3) _____

Everyone won't write a book to remove their Mask. Removing the Mask might be as simple as deciding to forgive. Removing the Mask starts with the decision, "I want it GONE!"

Forgiveness is a huge factor in the healing process. There are so many to forgive for what was done to us. The first person we must forgive is ourselves. That guilty must be erased. Your new recording must say, It Is Not My Fault. Say it and believe it.

There are abuses that we suffered from that have caused many damaging disorders. Not one disorder is greater than God. He is superior to any affliction. He is our Great Healer. His healing comes to those who ask for it. Just believe that He will heal all of your wounds, starting with your mind.

> Jeremiah 17:14 (NLT)
> *14 O Lord, if you heal me, I will be truly healed; if you save me, I will be truly saved. My praises are for you alone!*

Trusting God for healing from all of your diseases, afflictions and abuse is the greatest decision you can make. He will heal your every disorder and redeem it back into order. Just ask Him. It's really strange how the enemy, who comes only to steal, kill and destroy me, uses trickery (lies) such as:

- I can CONTROL what comes against me next.
- I can ignore it and it will go away.
- If I just give into it and it won't be as bad as the last time.
- And if that doesn't work, I can just numb it with whatever my choice of escape, be it drugs, alcohol, sex, etc.

Whatever the lie is, please hear my heart when I say this: it is a LIE! There is no future in handling things on your own. You are weak in our own strength, but you are made strong when you are in Christ Jesus.

- You are complete in Him.
- You are empowered to do, be, and have whatever it is He has for you, lacking in nothing.
- You are never alone.
- You have been bought with a price and that price is the blood of Jesus.
- You have been sealed with the Holy Spirit to protect you while you are waiting for your full redemption.

Like I said earlier, the devil comes only to steal, kill, and destroy, but Jesus came that you might have and enjoy your life (John 10:10). You are completely safe, secure, and protected with God.

It's time to stop fighting to be accepted by a world that has no real life in it, by people who are so self-absorbed that they didn't even recognize you had left the room. It's time for true acceptance. Acceptance in Christ Jesus doesn't just come as a religion but by being in a relationship with Him. Being a Christian isn't supposed to be about following after a bunch of rules or mandatory church attendance.

Having been a Christian for many years, I was attending this one church for over fifteen years. I was the leader of the youth ministry, teaching them Bible truths. I was an ordained minister, who seriously knew how to work a church program. I knew church, the ins and outs of it. But during that time of serving, if someone would have asked me who Jesus was, I wouldn't have been able to answer it fully. If someone would have asked me what the Bible, the written word, had to say about how loved I was and what it means to be redeemed, I wouldn't have been able to answer those questions. See, what I am saying is this, I knew church, I knew how to serve in a church. I played the role of being more of a Christian than I was, another (Mask). I was more knowledgeable, more saved (in actions) more righteous than others and more religious.

But in truth I didn't know what salvation really meant. It was a big punch in the belly to learn that just because I faithfully attended a church this did not make me a Christian or saved. I didn't know what being redeemed looked like. I was broken, bruised and hurt. I lived through fear, shame, guilt, bitterness and hatred. I hurt all the time. I got so frustrated with living the fake Christian life that I finally cried out to God for help! I told Him I needed more than this. I was so tired of people pleasing another (Mask), only to come up short and offended because there was never any pleasing them. I thought that with all the time and money that I was so faithful in giving, it made me more important than some. The haughtiness was so suffocating. Living a religious life was harder than living a righteous life, if you can believe that.

These feelings continued to weigh down on my mind and in my heart. I couldn't shake the immense heaviness of my heart and the great longing for an unburdened life. I was tired, overwhelmed, especially when I felt a tug on my heart that it was time to leave my church. There was nothing wrong with the church as far as what was going on with me. I chose not to learn of God for myself. If I can say anything to you it's this, don't let Christ be preached at you; go and search through the love letters "the Bible" that were written for us for yourself. Don't sit in a church and not grow in your relationship with Jesus. Don't get so busy with serving a man or woman, a position or title. You will find yourself serving and pleasing them more than spending time falling in love with Jesus. Fall deeper and deeper in love with Christ, and when you think you have fallen enough, fall some more. Know Him and the beauty of His resurrection (restoration to life). I had to come to myself and say to God there has to be more! I wanted to know more about Jesus Christ as my Lord and Savior.

I knew Jesus by name. I heard a lot about Him. Remember I was in church well over fifteen years where He was preached. But to release myself to be in a relationship with Him, I did not trust enough in Him to let that happen. To me that was just church lingo. I had to learn that seeking to know Him was not about religion, but it was about being in a relationship with Jesus Christ. Being a Christian is about being in a relationship with a Love that will never leave you nor forsake you. He will never lie to you. He will never take advantage of you or harm you. He does not condemn you for your past. Your past is just that: it is your past. Being <u>in Christ Jesus</u> you <u>are a new creation;</u> all <u>old things have passed away</u> (the old ways of thinking and living, the old lies that keep assaulting you in your mind and the wrong thoughts you have believed about yourself); and you are now a new CREATION!

Jesus offered Himself as the sacrificial payment for our sins. He took away our shame, pain and guilt. When we receive Him, His Holy Spirit comes and lives in us. Now that you are born again (repent of sin and receive Jesus as Savior) you are a new creation. You no longer have to jump through hoops trying to be good enough or clean enough to get God to love you. You belong to Him. He loves you and no one can take you from Him. You have been sealed with a promise from God and let me tell you He is a promise keeper. He does not expect you to travel this new road alone that is why He gave you His Holy Spirit. His job is to lead you in the way the Lord wants you to go. All you have to do is listen and obediently following His prompting. He knows the plans the Lord has for you and He alone knows how to get you there. Embrace your new life. Accept the new start up.

So, acceptance comes in three ways. You are accepted, accepted, accepted. The Father has accepted you. Jesus has accepted you and the Holy Spirit has accepted you. You have been accepted not once, but three times. You are accepted in the Beloved. In Ephesians 1:5-8a AMP it reads,

In love He predestined and lovingly planned for us to be adopted to Himself as (His own) children through Jesus Christ, in accordance with the kind intention and good pleasure of His will to the praise of His glorious grace and favor, which he so freely bestowed on us in the Beloved (His Son, Jesus Christ). In Him we have redemption (that is, our deliverance and salvation) through His blood (which paid the penalty for our sin and resulted in) the forgiveness and complete pardon of our sin, in accordance with the riches of His grace which he lavished on us.

To some of you who are reading this, I'm sure this is not a new word for you, but it is a NOW word for you. For those who do not understand, this means that God has bestowed (given, granted, awarded) His grace upon you. It means that God knows everything about you and through Jesus, you have been found highly favored. If you are accepted in Jesus, you have been accepted at the highest level and to the greatest degree possible. Jesus was rejected by men and died on the cross; therefore, he knows how you feel being rejected, abused, and neglected. He will never reject you.

This is the time for the greatest decision you will ever make for the improvement of your life. What kind of life did God intend for us to have? It certainly is not one of being reduced, cheapened, abused, molested, rejected, and assaulted. He offers unconditional love, infinite worth and value, wholeness, righteousness, peace, and joy – and that is just the beginning of His blessings for those who will believe and walk with Him through life. He has healing for you if you want it. But remember healing takes time; it's a process. It is also sometimes painful because you must let the old wounds be opened up in order to get the infection that is festering and poisoning your souls out of them.

God's plan from the beginning of your life still stand. It does not matter what Satan tried to kill. He is powerless to God. Because there is sin in this world and very sinful people God planned for Jesus to come and redeem us back to God. This is where salvation comes into play. What is salvation? Salvation is defined as being saved from or delivered from sin or harm. It means being saved from danger, evil, difficulty, and destruction. It's kind of like being rescued. Who is your Rescuer? Jesus and He alone is your rescuer.

There is no other god, person, or thing that can save you. Jesus said, "Let the little children come to me, and do not hinder the, for the kingdom of heaven belongs to such as these? (Matthew 19:14). You are the little children that Jesus is calling. Say yes! You are now saved! The Grace and Salvation of God are FREE!
"I thank my God always concerning you for the grace of God which was given to you by Christ Jesus" (1 Corinthians 1:4)

Let's be perfectly clear, the Grace we receive from God is FREE. We do not earn, accept, or reject it. The GRACE of God is ours as a FREE gift. We only learn of it "by Jesus Christ". And we are SAVED by the grace of God, it is also FREE. And we only learn it is ours "through Jesus Christ". "...the FREE GIFT of God is Eternal Life through Jesus Christ our Lord" (Romans 6:23b NASB) [5]

It doesn't matter what has happened to you don't let what happened be your identity. You are saved, set free of your past. Walk boldly into your new life. God has set before you a choice of life or death. Choose life. This new life comes with being complete in God. He is all powerful. Literally He restores you to greatness in Him. It does not matter about your past. It's all about your future in Him. God will pull you out of your unwanted, undeserved and unfair circumstances and bring you up to where it is He desires for you to be. Ask Him for your complete resurrected life in Him. So, to answer my earlier questions on how to rip off all the Masks you have worn for such a long time, it is this: give your life God. Again, this is not a religion, but a relationship that will never fail. Go forth and enjoy the journey to a new way of living. Go on, Love, Invest in, Value and Enjoy your life (L.I.V.E.)!

STRATEGY 3: EXPOSING THE PREDATOR

So far, we have discussed in Strategy 1 and 2 that it's not your fault and that it's important to remove the mask. While it isn't your fault you were molested, raped and or sex-trafficked, it is your decision to remove the Mask of shame, pain, and guilt.

In Strategy 3, we will talk about what it looks like to expose the molester by removing his/her mask. Before going too deep in the psyche of a molester, I must mention that I am not a psychologist or sociologist. I do not have "gist" behind my name at all. I am simply trying to share with you information that will help you in your healing process that helped me. By knowing the molester or predator and his or her tactics, this will give you a better understanding of what or who you were against.

Researching the following information gave me a greater understanding of the mind and actions of the Predator. I understand that as a child I never had a chance against the predators in my life. I pray that you too come to that same understanding. It's horrid that the abuse happened. It's even more horrific that this demonic, lying, lustful spirit still exists generations later. This kind of spirit attaches itself to a family line and prepares itself to destroy all that is good in that family lineage by taking out its most precious gift, the children.

Although I am writing to you young girl this victimization also happen to boys as well, their victimizing is it widely unreported. Those who are sexually abused as children are more susceptible to depression, eating disorders, suicidal behavior and drug and alcohol problems later in life; they are more likely to become victims of sexual assault as adults. [5] They have little to no self-worth. They give up their value to those around them, especially male attractions. They commit crimes to supply the needs for others. They do time for men out of a twisted sense of love. Their weaknesses are preyed upon because the predators in their lives know they have nowhere else to go.

The below story I am going to share is about a young girl named Deborah. I share this story for those of you who had been raised on or is currently in the foster care system. There is so much predatory behavior that goes on in this system. I don't have to tell you this especially if you are or were a foster child or worked in the field. Deborah's story is one that compiles several other stories that I have received from young girls who are now women in the correctional facility that were raised in the foster system.

Their stories speak of the predatory nature of some of the homes they entered. Now let me say here not all foster care parents are predators. And may God bless them. But to those who are all about the money and not about giving unconditional love and care to a broken child, then to you I say God forgive them. I share this story to remind those who are in the system and are getting ready to age out of the system. Debbie's story could have gone very wrong for her. It was difficult, but survivable. There were decisions made, consequences had. I say to you, please know that there is great life to be had once you are out of the system making your own choices.

Debbie was put in foster care at thirteen months old. She remained in foster care until she aged out at eighteen. She was given to several families until she was almost three. At age three she was given to this one family from my church. They had a couple other kids they were fostering at this time. Debbie was so chunky and bubbly I didn't understand why she hadn't been adopted by now. Well this family kept Debbie until she aged out of foster care at eighteen. I don't know why they did not adopt her, nor do I have to. She was involved in my youth group and was very active in high school. I just knew Debbie was college bound because she was smart and driven. Well on her eighteenth birthday, to my understanding, she was placed out of the foster care system, and that family who had raised this beauty young woman put her out of their home. Now before I go further, I don't know what all took place because Debbie did not tell me this on her own, but her friends who were in school and church told me. And to my understanding if you are still in high school at age eighteen the foster care system still supports you until you graduate.

After graduation and displacement Debbie's friends could not locate her because she had stopped hanging around with them and had stopped coming to church. And since I was in law enforcement, they came to me in hopes that I would know how to find her. Debbie's spirit was broken from the knowledge that she was going to be homeless in a few months so just gave up on ever going to college or doing anything goo. And I learned that she dropped out of school in her last trimester. She did not graduate from high school before she had disappeared. I was unable to find her since she was never in the system for any criminal activities. She did however resurface around the end of summer the following year. She showed up at the church one Sunday, sat in the back pews looking lost. The family that raised her was still attending our church but was not there on that particular Sunday. I wished they were because they would have seen what I saw. Debbie had apparently been doing drugs, because she appeared high and agitated. She looked and dressed differently. She looked neglected, and thrown away. Not smelly or dirty but just broken. When I saw her, I was excited to see her and to know she was alive. I watched as a couple of the youth girls went to her in excitement only to be turned away by her cold withdrawal. You can tell she was unable to fake excitement. Her eyes were darkened. There was no telling what she had gone through. Well she ended up leaving the church before the service was over. That was the last time I saw her until years later. I asked myself why didn't I go to her and throw my arms around her and let her know she was loved. No one did. We stared at her but did not embrace her.

The next time I heard about Debbie was when she had been arrested on drug charges. I actually had a chance to speak with her in jail. And after some awkwardness on my part, simply because the little girl that I once knew was gone and the young woman sitting before me was not comfortable letting me come too close to her. I wanted to embrace her but the place or time did not allow it And her embarrassment of my seeing her there did not help it. After a few more encounters she eventually broke down her wall and started talking to me. Come to find out she was doing time for this dude she was in love with. He was on parole and if he owned the charges he would have to go back to prison and leave her. Her answer told me everything. She had abandonment issues, rightfully so. The family that raised her did not love her or make her feel safe and apart of the family. She was a check to them. She was told by them on numerous occasions that once you turn eighteen and those checks stop coming in she will have to go. They told her by law they could not keep her after she reached the age of eighteen. She believed them. When you are told all of your life, that you are here but you don't belong here, that's a whole different type of predator. A predator that stole this young girl of love, safety and acceptance has a name also and that name is Rejection and Abandonment. How awful!

Debbie's story doesn't end terribly. She did her time and got her head straight about what and who is important in her life. While in jail she got her G.E.D. Once she finished her time she connected with some friends and went and stayed with them. She went College and got her degree and is now working for the State of California. (Yes, the State does hire people who have a criminal record. You can go to college if you have a criminal record. You can find employment even if you have a criminal record. All is not lost just because you have a criminal record.)

I said all of this to say that in Debbie's story there were several predators in her life. Only one was a sexual predator and his name was Kevin. And Kevin was the man she went to jail for. Here's how her story started after she disappeared.

Kevin saw her sitting in a park alone and hungry. It was her third day away from home. She was lost and a young girl who had nothing or no one. She was pretty sheltered in her raising. She trusted one of her friends she had kept in touch with, when she said she could come stay with her. Well after the third night the mother of her friend told her she would not be able to stay with them. She said Debbie needs to go home and make up with her parents. Her friend's mom didn't understand that Debbi couldn't go back there. Something happened there that made Debbie flee. She left before she turned eighteen. Debbie didn't understand, she thought it was all arranged for her to just move in there. Well her friend was still going to school and Debbie had to leave that morning. She had nowhere to go. She walked around all day until she ended up in the park. Kevin introduced himself to her. He was nice to her. He was cute too. As he talked to her she became at eased around him. He asked her if she was hungry and because she was starving, she said yes. He took her to Popeye's Chicken where she ate and got her fill.

It was getting dark now, so he asked her if she had a place to stay. At first, she told him yes, and then with tears in her eyes she told him no. He told her he had a friend, who was a girl and that he could call her to see if she would let her sleep on her couch for the night. The friend said yes and he drove her over to this friend, whose name was Cherry. Cherry was alright toward her at first. They all sat around and talked, drank and they (Cherry and Kevin) started smoking dope. They offered it to her and in fear of being laughed at or worst put out, she started smoking. Everything changed from there. Kevin started touching her on her legs, just rubbing them at first. She was drunk and high so her ability to see what was coming was very foggy. Cherry was sitting in the chair next to the couch. Kevin laid her down on the couch and took off her pants and undies. She was laying there exposed. She remembers both Kevin and Cherry touching her all over. She was raped that night by both.

When she woke up Cherry was in her room and Kevin was asleep in the chair next to the couch. There was a towel thrown over her lower half, but her breast area was exposed. She grabbed at them attempting to cover up. There was little light in the room, but she did find her cloths on the floor near her. She tried to get dressed without waking anyone up, but Kevin did wake up. He asked her where she was going. She said she had to go home. He reminded her that she said she had nowhere to live. He told her he had a lot of fun with her tonight and she could stay with him if she wanted. He told her she was beautiful and special. He told her he will take care of her and that he loved her. She believed him. She wanted to be loved. She was afraid of being alone. She didn't know what love really looked like, but she wanted it. She stayed with Cherry for about a week and then she moved in with Kevin. He was renting a room from a friend. Things were cool at first, but they got bad really quickly. Kevin wasn't really working he sold a little dope here and there. He was having trouble with his friend for moving her in his room. They had to move in a motel that they paid daily to live there. His anger grew. He became abusive to her and raped her whenever he wanted. And beat on her when she would refuse. She lived in fear for almost one year.

Kevin sold drugs sometimes when money was low. He talked about her making quick money for them by sleeping with some guys he knew. She refused and that is when he would really rape and beat on her. He finally got caught with drugs in the car. They were pulled over and with fear in his eyes he told her if the police found his stash she was to say it was hers. If she loved him she had to do this or he would go to prison and leave her. You know the rest of the story. The Predator preyed on his prey and conquered.

I will now attempt to explain the difference between the Predator and Prey. I want you to see from the story above there is so many devices Kevin used to manipulate his way over Debbie's life. Fear of abandonment and rejection is key here. So read carefully the below facts that I learned and feel a great need to share. First what is a Predator? What is a Prey? Which one are you? Ask God to give you open eyes so that you can Cleary see and understand the truth when you say, "It is not my fault."

PREDATOR VS. PREY

I would like to first define the difference between Predator and Prey. Here is my understanding. When we look at the predator role in the ecosystem (an ecosystem is all the plants and animals that live in a particular area having complex relationships between them and their environment) the energy flow takes place through prey and predator interactions. Predator always adapts to maximize its capabilities to kill the prey; on the other hand, prey always adapts and tries to get away from its predators as much as possible via various means.

Predator's main role in the ecosystem is to maintain the prey population, (he is in control who comes and who goes) and they improve the biodiversity (the variety of each species) by preventing a single species from becoming dominant. Usually, the prey is the submissive organism of the predator- prey interaction. [6]

SEXUAL PREDATOR

So now let's take the same definition of a Predator and expound towards Sexual Predatory behavior. A sexual predator is a person seen who committed a sexually violent offense and especially one who is likely (as because of mental abnormality or a psychological disorder) to commit more sexual offenses. Sexual Predators commit sex crimes, such as rape or child molestation or other kinds of sexual abuse such as trafficking others for monetary purposes without remorse. Similar to how a predator hunts down its prey, the sexual predator is thought to "hunt" for his or her sex victim in that same aggressive manner. [7]

Nowadays, predators comes at the prey in many different forms. People who habitually engage in internet discussions of a sexual nature with minors are considered sexual predators. Aside from trying to lure children into offline meetings, predators are also on the lookout for photos or conversations of a sexual nature. They also use children to secure information they can use later for other attacks, such as the best way to get into a school's dormitory or whether a group of kids often play outside without adult supervision.

According to Loreen Olson, an Associate Professor in the Communication Studies at the University of North Carolina stated, "Our children are our greatest gift and our greatest responsibility. The fact that they could be abused in any way, shape or form is horrific-- both in the moment of the abuse and in the long-term effect. It's a social problem with grave consequences that is prevalent and needs attention. It's incomprehensible, but it's happening. The sexual abuse of children has dramatic negative consequences to their emotional well-being throughout their lives." [8]

If you are a parent of a victimized child or you were victimized, the following information will equip you in spotting the tricks, traps and tools the Predator uses.

The University of Missouri researchers along with Dr. Olson, are beginning to understand the communication process by which predators lure victims into a web of entrapment. This information could better equip parents, schools, churches and community members to prevent, or at least interrupt, the escalation of child sexual abuse. In order for the process of entrapment to take place, the predator must first gain access to the potential prey through various exploitive means. Olson and her team identified several communicative elements in the cycle of entrapment, including the core phenomenon of "deceptive trust development."

Deceptive trust development describes the predator's ability to build a trusting relationship with the victim in order to improve the likelihood of a sexual encounter. Deceptive trust development is central to other manipulative strategies used by the predator such as grooming. Grooming sets the stage for abuse by desensitizing the victim to sexual contact. Grooming may include activities such as sitting on a child's bed and watching them get into their bedclothes; "accidentally" touching the child inappropriately; showing the child pornographic images; and making contact or sex play with implicit sexual suggestions.

As predators are grooming their preys and building deceptive trust, they also work to isolate them both physically and emotionally from their support network. Isolation strategies may include offers to babysit, giving the child a ride home, and taking advantage of fragile family and friend relationships. Isolation causes the prey to become more and more dependent on the predator.

A third strategy is approach, which is the initial physical contact or verbal lead-ins that occur just prior to the sexual act. Examples of approach strategies include suggestions to play sex games, more explicit discussions about sexual issues, giving a child a "rubdown," bathing or undressing a child, and instigating wrestling and other physical games as a means to escalate sexual physical contact.

Olson, and her co-authors analyzed existing published material on pedophilia and child sexual abuse and proposed their theory that explains the communication process used by child sexual predators. Their theory of luring communication is part of a new area of study which Olson calls "the communication of deviance. "The more we know about how these adults are entrapping children and building a sexual relationship with them, the better we can either intervene and stop the cycle from happening, or de-escalate it,"[9]

This is why this book is written! The above information is true to the core. This is why I added this study in the Strategy. It is so important for you to see that as Prey, there was no way you or I could have known we were headed for victimization. IT IS AND WAS NOT YOUR FAULT! So, where do we go from here?
EDUCATION AND EXPOSURE
The following information will aid you and your child in Ripping off the Mask of the Monster! It's all about early detection, elimination and full exposure. Teaching children in schools about sexual abuse may help them report abuse. Children who are taught about preventing sexual abuse at school are more likely than others to tell an adult if they had, or were actually experiencing sexual

abuse. In many countries, children are taught how to recognize, react to, and report abuse situations through school-based programs designed to help prevent sexual abuse. [10] I do not know if this is or isn't true here in the United States.

Teaching your child and educating yourself about Sexual Predators is SO NEEDED!

The internet is one source in getting information that can aid you. Sexual Molestation occurs mainly between 12 to 17 years old, roughly 40 percent of girls and 17 percent of boys reported they had experienced at least one type of child sexual abuse. Relative to boys, sexual abuse without physical contact was reported twice as often in girls and sexual abuse with physical contact without penetration three times more often. Both genders reported sexual molestation as the most frequent form of abuse. This form of sexual molestation was experienced by roughly 28 percent of girls over the course of their lifetimes and by almost 10 percent of boys. At just under 15 percent for girls versus 5 percent for boys, "molested verbally or by e-mail/text message" was the second most common form of abuse. Just under 12 percent of the surveyed girls and 4 percent of the surveyed boys reported having been kissed or touched against their will. Approximately 2.5 percent of the girls had already experienced sexual molestation with penetration (vaginal, oral, anal or other); among boys, this figure was 0.6 percent.

Disturbing data, I do agree. But very informative. The vast amount of cases that are reported every year is astounding. About 3.5 million cases of child abuse are reported in the United States every year. Similarly, alarming situations exist in many other countries. Abused children often suffer from emotional and behavioral problems, which can later develop into sexual dysfunction, anxiety, promiscuity, vulnerability to repeated victimization, depression, substance abuse and suicidal ideologies.

Through further research I found that children responded to the abuse in two general ways. In physical abuse cases, which are cases where any intentional act that causes injury or trauma to another person. In these cases the children tended to be accommodating -- they accepted and tried to minimize the severity of the abuse. On the other hand, children reporting sexual abuse, also referred to as molestation, which is abuse where undesired sexual behavior by one person upon another by use of force. These victims tend to fight back. But when the alleged sexual abuse was severe, the children tended to act like physical abuse victims, accommodating the abuser. Older children, they found, were more likely to fight than younger ones. But surprisingly, the frequency of the abuse, familiarity with the abuser, and the child's gender did not significantly affect how the children responded.

When a man was accused of sexually abusing his young daughter, it was hard for many people to believe -- a neighbor reported seeing the girl sitting and drinking hot chocolate with her father every morning, laughing, smiling, and looking relaxed. Such cases are not exceptional, however. Children react to sexual and physical abuse in unpredictable ways, making it hard to discern the clues. (11)

The majority were victimized by juvenile predators.

Just over half of the female victims and more than 70 percent of the male victims reported that they had been abused by a juvenile predator. Furthermore, most of the victims of sexual abuse with physical contact knew the predator -- for instance, they were siblings, partners, peers, or acquaintances. What does this mean? Most juvenile predators were victims themselves. Not excusing their conduct, but explaining it. They come from a dysfunctional life style. Your child befriends this person only to become their victim. It is still an entrapment that I previously mentioned.

How the Predator grooming process work? Here is how the Predator con you and your child. In most child sexual molestation cases, the Predator 'grooms' their victims and the victim's parents before the abuse, so that disclosure of the abuse is less likely and/or less believable. Here are some ways that you can identify grooming tendencies and prevent child sexual molestation.

Sexual predators have several tools at their disposal to carry out their sickening abuses on children; fear, isolation, power, and silence are major tactics used by molesters. Perhaps the most effective and deceptive tool predators' use is the Grooming Process to prepare their victims for an eventual abuse. Specifically, grooming is the tactic of gradually and methodically building trust with a child – and the adults around them – to gain increased access and alone time with their future victim. This can come in several forms; the predator may assume a caring role in the child's life –

behaviors such as favoritism, granting special privileges are just a couple forms that the 'caring' role is assumed by the predator. (12)

This is what happened with Mr. John and me. He used this tactic on my mom and me like the expert Predator he was. After friending our family, he had full access to me anytime he desired. And because we were well groomed it was never a question of whether I went with him or not until I got older and made myself unavailable. Here's a key for you parents: do not trust anyone with full access to you children, no matter how in need you are. Remember, our children are our greatest gift and our greatest responsibility.

You have to ask yourself this question, "how can a person do this to a child?" The question to ask is not "how" a person could do this; after all, sexual predators are very similar to con-artists, and will look for any advantage to increase their chances of successfully abusing a child. The real question is "what" the sexual predator gains by grooming their future victim. They can gain significant advantages, such as reducing disclosure, reducing the likelihood of the child being believed, reducing detection, manipulate adult perception of the child, and convince the child into being a cooperative participant. In each element of the grooming process, the predator will also use their ability to charm and be likeable; it's the most effective way to get a child to trust them, and also the easiest way for adults to be unassuming at first, and possibly even support the molester during allegations.

It's important to recognize that grooming is an incremental process, with noticeable stages prior to the occurring of the actual abuse. One of the better representations of this cycle is:

1. Targeting the prey: In this phase, the predator will 'size up' their prey. Specifically, the predator is looking for vulnerabilities such as physical or mental disabilities, single-parent/low income families, low self-confidence, or emotional neediness. They will look in places with high concentrations of children – schools, churches, malls, playgrounds etc.
2. Gain trust: After a predator has selected their prey, they will begin to gather information about them and

place themselves in areas where they can give their future victim attention.
3. Fill a need: Once a predator gains initial access to their prey, they can look for gaps in supervision to exploit, and 'be there' for the child when the parent is unable to (e.g. give the child a ride home).
4. Isolation: Now that the predator has found a way to maintain a routine relationship with the prey (and parents), they will seek ways to spend alone time with the prey (e.g. babysitting, give a ride, tutoring, or special trips).
5. Make the relationship sexual: The predator makes their move on their prey when they are able to isolate them, and does so by preying on the child's natural curiosity to advance their sexual agendas.
6. Maintain control: Once the molestation occurs, the predator will do all they can to keep the prey silent and available for continued abuse. This control can come in the form of verbal threats (e.g. nobody will believe you), or physical threats (e.g. I will kill you and your family if you tell).

Remember also there is no typical description of a sexual predator; they come from all genders, races, occupations, and relation to the child. Here are some statements from convicted child molesters – experts in their own right – that explain just "how" they operated:

- "Parents are naive; they are worried about strangers…they should be worried about their brother- in-law."
- "I was disabled and groomed the parents into having their children help me. No one thought a disabled person could be an abuser."
- "Parents are to blame if they don't teach their children about sex. I used that to my advantage by teaching them myself."

As you can tell, the predator's tactics are deceitful in nature, tricky to separate from a genuine relationship, and often without the ability to confront the predator in person. What can a parent do then, to prevent their child from becoming the next abuse statistics?

- Early Education: All conversations about how to prevent child sexual abuse must start with educating children at a young age about their 'private' parts, the difference between appropriate and inappropriate touching, and what to do when a predator attempts to cross the line. Having this conversation will make your child a much harder target for would-be predators.
- Maximize Supervision: As much as possible, try to personally supervise your child's time away from school; if your child is slated to attend a field trip and if you can afford to, volunteer to chaperone the trip. In the event you are unable to personally supervise your child, ensure a trusted family member or friend does.
- Identify Sex Offenders Near You: Megan's Law is enacted in all 50 states; in California, it allows you to use several online databases and applications to locate sex offenders near your home, your child's school, or extracurricular activities.
- Love Your Child: This is second nature to most of us; however, a predator can sniff out when a child hasn't received enough attention from their parents, and will act to fill that void for you. Take time out of your busy schedule to be there for your child, let him or her know that you love them, and spend time with them – even if their idea of fun seems silly. Spending time with your child is more important than that project you've been working on, or that video game you're playing with your friends, or that TV show on your DVR, or watching a sporting event, or spending time on Facebook or any other social media.
- Know the Warning Signs: Knowing the mood shifts or irregular behaviors associated with a child's sexualized relationship with the predator is crucial to

putting a stop to further abuse, and might prevent it altogether.

In conclusion, early and consistent engagement by parents is the best method to preventing children from being groomed by a sexual predator. These tips and methods are useful to identify where the child might be in the grooming process, and also allow somebody to step in and stop an abuse from happening. [13]

TALKING TO YOUR CHILD ABOUT MOLESTATION

Sexual molestation can be a very difficult topic to discuss with others. This is especially true when it comes to talking about sexual abuse with your children.

Though parents are frequently confronted by messages about the dangers of sexual abuse and molestation, they receive little advice about how to bring up this sensitive subject with their kids. This section of Strategy 3 will address how to talk about sexual abuse with your children.

Use visual aids such as the video, My Body Belongs to Me. Talk to your child about sexuality and sexual abuse in age-appropriate terms.

When you talk to your children about sexuality and sexual abuse, you should use age-appropriate terms for body parts and other concepts.

Ideally, you should teach your children the anatomical terms for their body parts, rather than using nicknames or slang terms. It is important to teach children the proper names of their body parts so that they can ask questions and express concerns about those body parts. Nicknames and slang terms may obscure a child's legitimate concerns about inappropriate touching. If using anatomical terms makes you uncomfortable, try teaching your child that his or her "private parts" are those body parts that are covered by underwear or a swimsuit.

Frame the conversation around "safety," rather than "abuse." Tell your child that you want to have a discussion about safety and their bodies. Explain the difference between safe touching (such as being examined at the doctor's office) and unsafe touching (inappropriate tickling or fondling). Tell your child that some people may try to touch him or her in a way that is unsafe, or causes feelings of discomfort, sadness, anger, or confusion. Tell your child that if this ever happens, he or she should tell you right away and that he or she will not get in trouble for doing so.

Maintain an open dialogue with your children, and make it clear that they are never to blame for inappropriate touching. Tell your children that it is okay to say "no" to adults in situations where they feel uncomfortable. [14]

IF YOU ARE CONCERNED ABOUT THE POSSIBILITY OF SEXUAL ABUSE, TALK TO YOUR CHILD IN A NON-JUDGMENTAL WAY.

If you are concerned that your child may have been sexually abused, you should have a candid conversation with him or her as soon as possible. Take these steps to ensure that your child feels comfortable discussing what may have happened with you:

- Choose a time and place carefully. Have this conversation with your child at a time when you won't be rushed and in a place where he or she feels comfortable. Never ask your child about sexual abuse in front of the abuser.
- Ask your child if anyone has been touching them in an unsafe way, or in a way that makes him or her feel uncomfortable. It is important to understand that asking your child if someone is hurting him or her may not lead to the information you are looking for. Because sexual abuse can feel good to the victim, a child may not know how to answer this question.
- Use a non-judgmental tone when talking to your child about sexual abuse. Reassure him or her that they will not get in trouble for anything that they tell you. Try to remain calm, even if your child comes forward with allegations of sexual abuse. A child may misinterpret your anger at the abuser as anger at him or her.
- Tell your child that it is okay to divulge a secret, even if an adult has made them promise not to do so. Many abusers tell their victims that what happened between them is a secret, relying on a child's willingness to keep quiet.

- Believe your child. Children rarely make false allegations of sexual abuse. You can always consult with a trusted professional, such as a pediatrician, therapist, or law enforcement officer, who is experienced in handling allegations of sexual abuse.
- If your child does not reveal sexual abuse, but your suspicions persist, follow up with your child. Remind your child that you are always available to talk about his or her safety, and that you will do whatever it takes to keep your child safe.
- Take abuse allegations seriously. If your child tells you that he or she has been abused, contact the authorities right away. Do not contact the abuser directly, or the institution where the abuse took place (such as a school or church).

Discussing sexual abuse with your children can be extremely challenging. However, maintaining an open dialogue about sexual abuse can be critical in preventing abuse from occurring or continuing. If you believe that your child may have been the victim of child sexual abuse, an honest, non-adversarial conversation is the first step in getting your child the help that he or she needs.[15]

ADDITIONAL RESOURCES:
1. Local: The Sacramento Regional Family Justice Center, 3701 Power Inn Road, Suite 3100, Sacramento, Ca 95826. (916)-875-4673 one-Stop support
2. National Sexual Assault Hotline. Free. Confidential. 24/7. Call 800-656- 4673
3. HOPE FOR SURVIVORS OF CHILD MOLESTATION
4. Rape, Abuse & Incest National Network (RAINN) at (800) 656-HOPE

STRATEGY 4: WHO'S TO BLAME?

Whenever I attempt to share my testimony and faith with someone who has been victimized by a predator, they usually come back with this angry question, "Where was God? Why did He allow it to happen to you? Why did He allow it to happen to me?"

My answer was and always will be, "He was right there with me back then as He is with me right now. He never left me for one second. I don't know why it had to happen to me, but I am thankful that He bought me through those most horrific experiences of my life. He is now using my experience to help someone who is still struggling with the effects of being a victim to their past and or present."

I'm telling you now, it does not have to affect your future. Don't let it!

What does it mean to blame others? According to the dictionary, it means to "assign responsibility for a fault or wrong." In other words, who should be held responsible, accountable, liable, and guilty for the wrong done? When it comes to sexual assault, the answer is the predator.

So many people failed to protect me during those years. I don't believe my mama would have knowingly allowed me to go with them if she had known what they were doing to me. Growing older, it was difficult for me to see who was at fault for the assaults. One thing I know for sure is that it wasn't my Fault! But the predators are the only ones to blame. We also have an enemy that wants to take us all out of God's awesome promise for us.

This enemy is real. He is bad! He has a deadly agenda and that agenda is to steal your future, kill your destiny and destroy you! That enemy's name is Satan. He is the father of all evil. He uses other predators to carry out his malicious evil attacks. He wants to destroy as many OF US girls as possible.

His plan started in the Book of Genesis in the Garden of Eden. This garden was created by God for His creation Man (humans). It was a perfect place. God then place man in there. Man had no needs outside the garden. God does not make mistakes. Please be sure you understand that. God gives man free will and it is that free will that often times make the mistakes.

Here is where the "Fall of Man" came about. Genesis 3:1-13 NIV, in summary speaks of Satan conversing with Eve, deceiving her with tricks of words and eye lusting, and resulting in her being disobedience to God's commands. Here is where she and her husband Adam's decision to be disobedience to God brought sin and death to the world. Give Genesis chapter 3 a full read and you will get a better understanding of how Satan worked. You will also find he knows the truth that you and I are very powerful. This is why he tries so hard to take us out by using what makes us feel the worst about ourselves. By raping us of our self-worth and murdering our true beauty.

Why Me? I asked myself that question more times than I can count. Well as I said earlier, It's Not Your Fault! It's most likely the fault of your parents and their parents and the parents before them. It is called "Generational Curse", which means curses that are spiritual (demonic) bondages or tendencies for sinful behaviors that are passed down from one generation to another. biblicalcounselingdatabase.net/generational-curses/[16]

This all goes back to Adam and Eve's decision to disobey God and their disobedience resulted in Sin. So don't think it strange that we suffer from the sins of others as well as the sins of our own. We are living in a fallen world. So think about it, if you come from a family that suffers from alcohol, drugs, gambling, and eating addictions, sexual and physical abuses or plan oh dysfunctions that are the results of parents, generations ago, that has allowed a demonic spirit to connect spiritually with their family line. This is real and it will continue moving to the next generation (that's your children), if it is not dealt with. You must be healed of these curses, and that is how you protect your family and break them. You cannot break them on your own.

Through God's grace you can be healed from the sins of others and forgive those who have hurt you. I remember long ago praying to God to heal my land (me) and to protect my generations to come. See there was a spiritual demonic curse of molestation on my family line. There is years and years of sexual abuse against children, especially the girl child, from years past. Remember earlier I said I thought it was "Normalcy" to have to have sex with these men. Everyone was getting it done to them, so why not me? Well as an adult I prayed for the breaking of all curses off me and my family, but what I didn't do was give myself and the sins of my parents fully to God. I did the religious thing of praying, but not surrendering. There is nothing wrong with praying, but if you are not willing to release yourself totally to God that sin isn't going to go anywhere.

Years later as an adult you'll find out that that same old demonic spirit is still attacking your family line. It is heartbreaking to say the lease. But it is never too late to surrender yourself and family before the Lord and break the curse connection of demons, whatever the curse may be. By surrendering to God, which can seem hard and scary but well worth it, is the only way to get real freedom and healing from the generational curses that affects our lives. God loves us so much that He offers us total healing from all abuses. He gives us a new restored life free from all past sins and curses. God desires to give us so much of what He has for us all we have to do is receive it from Him.

There are many promises from God in His Word, the Bible, for you and every one of them are true. So to get free from generational curses is simply surrendering and submitting to God's will and receiving healing and freedom from your past and the past sins of others. There is a great teaching on breaking generational curse by Michael Bradley [17], https://www.bible-knowledge.com/six-steps-to-breaking-a-generational-curse. I would strongly encourage you to look it up. Also I would say get help through your church (if you belong to one) or Christian counseling. You can also get help through GAPMIN.

All mentioned resources are great for you. I seek counseling through my church and it helped me out a lot. It was so beneficial to me it made me want to help others so much so that I went to Bible college and became a Certified Christian counselor. The best way to reassure yourself that all these promises are for you is to make sure you are rightly connected. Your right connection comes from receiving Jesus Christ as your Lord and Savior. Believing by faith that He is for you and He got you. Believing by faith that real life is just one decision away. This new decision to reach out to Jesus comes with a promise that He will change your life. He will make you brand new. New life is now for you to have.

Have you ever wondered if you would ever feel different than you do right now? As you look back over your life and look at the decisions and mistakes you have made, you wonder not only if any human being would ever love you but if possible God will ever love you? The answer is Yes, God can and does love you. He gave us His most precious gift ever!

Understand that Jesus is described as your High Priest who has been touched by the feelings of your infirmities. He understands your failures and your hurts. He understands you have been rejected. He is intimately acquainted with your pain and your sorrow. He has come not looking for those who has done it all right, he has come looking for you who has sinned. Who has been disappointed? Who just can't seem to do it right? Jesus has come for you. He understands and hears the pain that is locked up in your heart. He sees your face and your tears. He says to you, give Me a chance, "come unto me all who are heavy laden, I want to give you my rest and peace (Matthew 11:28-29 NLT)." I know your heart has been broken. He understands that you have been disappointed and mishandled, sometimes you position yourselves to be misused.

It is time for you to rise up and give Jesus a chance. He understands the storm of life. He understands you want to take a chance one last time. Step away from your old life and step into your destiny. There is nothing done to that will ever keep God from loving you.

There are silent questions that you are asking yourself, "Will I always hurt? Will I always be disappointed? Is there a place that I can go to find true peace? The answer is a resounding Yes to every question! His name is Jesus! It doesn't matter how much dirt you have done (your sin), or the dirt that has been done to you, "For everyone has sinned; we all fall short of God's glorious standard. He is not afraid of you or your sin. Peace is only found in Jesus Christ. Today is your day for Salvation! Reach out to Him because He is reaching out for you.

Your deliverance and salvation is but one prayer away. He said whoever calls on Him shall be saved! Romans 10:13 says, for "whoever calls on the name of the Lord shall be saved." Now is the time of your SALVATION! I know there is fear in making this decision. But God says in Isaiah 41:13 (NKJV) "For I, the Lord your God, will hold your right hand, Saying to you, Fear Not, I will help you." God is all powerful. Again there is no failure in Him. "And God is able to make all grace abound toward you, that you, always having all sufficiency in all things, may have an abundance for every good work. 2 Corinthians 9:8 (NKJV). Only God can heal and only God can save for in Jeremiah 17:14 says, Heal me, O lord, and I shall be healed; Save me , and I shall be saved, For You are my praise."

There's this beautiful song I love to listen to, it's called "Reach Out for Jesus," by Bishop David G. Evans [18]

> *With a full understanding of who you are in Christ will help you*
> *desire a better life for yourself.*
> *This life in Christ is not something we work for or can buy or can*
> *be good enough to deserve it.*
> *This life in Christ is a free Gift from God.*
> *Freedom that will restore you back in a relationship with Him.*
> *Which is still all part of God's plan for us.*
> *Jesus said He is the Way.*
> *He will show you the Way.*

Here is where you have to make the decision that is best for you. I can tell you this; if you make the decision to live for Christ then you will be making the best decision of your life. If this is for you, read the confession below and believe it with all your heart, mind and soul.

This is the entire plan that will bring freedom and salvation to you. Confessing these words and believing your confession will be your new life. Go forward not back. Stop looking back at that old dead, abused, or rejected person and look forward to being able to L.I.V.E.

Your New Confession

- Step 1 – Admit you have sinned. Believe on Jesus. Confess Christ privately and publicly. We have all done, thought or said bad things, which the Bible calls "sin." The Bible says, "For all have sinned and fall short of the glory of God" (Romans 3:23 ESV). The result of sin is death, spiritual separation from God (Romans 6:23).
- Step 2 – Know that God loves you and has purpose and a plan for you! The Lord says, "For I know the plans and thoughts that I have for you, says the LORD, plans for peace and well-being and not for disaster to give you a future and a hope." (Jeremiah 29:11 AMP). The Bible says, "God so loved the world that He gave His one and only Son, [Jesus Christ], that whoever believes in Him shall not perish, but have eternal life" (John 3:16- 17 NIV). Jesus said, "I came that they may have life and have it abundantly"—a complete life full of purpose (John 10:10).
- Step 3 – Know that God sent His Son to die for your sins! Jesus died in our place so we could have a relationship with God and be with Him forever. "God demonstrates His own love toward us, in that while we were yet sinners, Christ died for us" (Romans 5:8). But it didn't end with His death on the cross. He rose again and still lives! "Christ died for our sins ... He was buried ... He was raised on the third day, according to the Scriptures" (1 Corinthians 15:3-4). Jesus is the only way to God. Jesus said, "I am the way, and the truth, and the life; no one comes to the Father, but through Me" (John 14:6).
- Step 4 – Make the choice: Would you like to receive God's forgiveness? We can't earn salvation; we are saved by God's grace when we have faith in His Son, Jesus Christ. All you

have to do is believe you are a sinner that Christ died for your sins, and ask His forgiveness. Then turn from your sins—that's called repentance. Jesus Christ knows you and loves you. He sees you. What matters to Him is the attitude of your heart, your honesty. I suggest praying the following prayer to accept Christ as your Savior: "Dear God, I know I'm a sinner, and I ask for your forgiveness. I believe Jesus Christ is Your Son. I believe that He died for my sins and that you raised Him to life. I want to trust Him as my Savior and follow Him as Lord, from this day forward. Guide my life and help me to do your will. I pray this in the name of Jesus. Amen."

What happens now? It's time to make some mindset changes. If you change what you believe, you will change what you desire. If you change what you desire, you will change what you do.

How do you do this? First allow the Holy Spirit to lead you to a bible teaching and believing church, red and study God's Word. There are so many Bible studies that are available to you online, in churches or through GAPMIN. Get to know others that believe the Word of God like you do. We call this a community. In the back of this book I have provided you point of contact information for GAPMINistries. Please feel free to contact us. We are available to assist you with walking out your success story.

This Scripture below gives you a greater understanding of your new position in Christ. Meditate on this truth and the many other truths that are in God's Word that will help you understand the power and authority you can now operate in.

> *"For we are His workmanship [His own master work, a work of art], created in Christ Jesus [reborn from above--spiritually transformed, renewed, ready to be used] for good works, which God prepared [for us] beforehand [taking paths which He set], so that we would walk in them [living the good life which He prearranged and made ready for us]." (Ephesians 2:10 AMP).*

Now to be able to stand in this truth you will need to live by the Spirit. What does this mean? You must trust God's Holy

Spirit (His own Spirit) as your Guide. He is your Helper, teacher, counselor and true coach.

Now, wherever you are, the Holy Spirit is with you, meaning you are never alone. You can lean on Him and receive guidance, wisdom, and counsel at any time. You don't have to try to figure this new life in Christ out on your own. Make sure you don't do the religious thing by adding a little Jesus to your troubled life; give your new life fully over to Jesus.

As a new Christian you are never to rely on your own limited understanding and flawed wisdom, desperately hoping that things will turn out all right. God never meant for you to live like that. Jesus is the Good Shepherd. The Holy Spirit is a Friend and a divine Counselor. He is right there by your side. Listen for Him, He will lead you into all truth. God is your Guide and His Word is a lamp unto your feet, providing direction. Receive the Holy Spirit as your Advocate and Helper today. He is near and ready to guide you.

> *"However, when He, the Spirit of truth, has come, He will guide you into all truth; for He will not speak on His own authority, but whatever He hears He will speak; and He will tell you things to come." (John 16:13 NKJV)*

By becoming empowered by the Spirit of God you can overcome the past, present and future life's pain. You can be equipped and not allow the abuse to become your identity.

Read Bayou's story and see if you can see yourself in it.

> *It all started with me as a little girl, the favorite one of the house was my little sister. Everyone always saw the bad in me. When in reality I never would do anything wrong. In fact I would always take my little sister's fault on myself so she would not get into trouble, I was already 10 or 11 years old and I would still get beat up badly by my mother. Every night I would cry myself to sleep. Also wondering why was I born into this family, why not a normal family? I mean I really wasn't asking for much. Just wanted to be able to go outside and play with friends. We weren't allowed to play outside, stay after school in the after school programs or anything. Watching other families and how they treated their kids always made me feel sad and unwanted in this world.*
>
> *I never had a good relationship with my parents; well my dad is just an alcoholic, till this day. He never really participated in our lives like that. With him it always was him working not being home and when he would come home he would go straight for his alcohol bottle, chug it.*

Straight afterwards he would either argue with my mom or eat and go straight to bed. And, well my relationship with my mom has always been not so great. I was really not able to talk with her about literally nothing. I always wished she would be that mom that could be my best friend that I would be able to talk with about everything just like every person I knew were with their mom. Well that never happened.

My sister was my mom's favorite which left me out. I felt alone, unwanted, in the wrong place, not loved. And that wasn't all, to top it off, I was being bullied at school. All of this happening to me and I had no one to talk too. At several different occasion i would lock myself in my room and cut myself and cry and wonder why was all this happening to me and why was God being so unfair to me. What did I ever do wrong? Until one day my mom passed all her limits, I was 13, and for a small thing I did, she beat me and dragged me by my hair across the whole damn apartment. I was yelling and crying I will never forget that day. I locked myself in my room and cried all day. The next day after we got out of school and came home, for not wanting to do my homework at the moment, my grandpa grabbed his belt and came toward me. I ran out the door and hid behind a bush. Because there was no way they would beat me up outside. I was there for at least 30 minutes before I decided to go back home. When I went inside I got yelled at by my mom and beat again.

I was so tired of life and my so called family at this point. I decided to pack some clothes and once everyone was asleep I decide to jump out my bedroom window with some clothing, and decided to never come back. I was only 13, walking in the middle of the night with a bag in my hands and no money. I walked to one of my friend's houses that I went to school with. I told her if I was able to spend the night at her house because I was having problems at my house. She said yes and she told her mom that we were having a sleepover since it was a Friday night. And she was okay with that.

While my friend was asleep, I was already thinking about where I was going to go because for sure I was not going back at all. The next morning, my friend gave me some money that she had been saving which was enough for me to buy a cell phone. We walked and bought one, and came back to her house, meanwhile her mom was still at work. I logged onto Myspace and got contact info of all my friends and my Myspace friends, which did not know them like that but I considered them my friends since I would talk to them every day. I had to figure out where was I going to go since Sunday was the next day and I would have to leave my friend's house otherwise her mom would notice that something was wrong.

I contacted one of my friends he was 20 years old at that time. He was actually one of my cousin's friends I told him I had nowhere to go, he said he was able to help me by getting me a night at a hotel since he wasn't working much. He told me to meet him at a park that was close by to where I was at. Sunday morning I walked to the park and waited until he showed up. When he showed up he came with a friend that I did not know, but I had seen him with my cousin before once or twice. We got to the hotel; I waited in the car while they got to the hotel since I was a minor. They came back to the car with the card to the hotel room. This was my first time being at a hotel. He walked me to the room. His friend tagged alone. We all sat on the bed and talked. His friend that tagged along was just quiet. He asked me if my cousin knew what was going on. I told him no. He asked me if I knew where I was going to go the next day. I told him, not yet I'll figure it out. I lied to him and told him I might go back home just so he wouldn't worry since he felt bad he was only able to help out for one night.

He asked me if I ate yet? And I hadn't, and I was starving. He asked me what I wanted. I told him tacos even though the restaurant was on the other side of town but that was the only fast food I ever tasted because my dad would bring it home sometimes. He said yea that it was totally fine. He said they would be back. He told his friend lets go, but his friend told him that he would stay so that way they don't tell me anything about room. So I didn't think anything of it. He said ok, he will be right back. Only if I knew, only if he knew what his friend was up too and why he wanted to stay. After he left, about two minutes his friend got up from the chair he was sitting in. I thought he was going to the restroom. I was on the bed watching TV, but now he came directly toward me. It thought maybe he was going to ask me something but no I was wrong. He pushed me hard into the bed and slapped me super hard. I was in shock, crying and yelling. I had no idea what I did wrong now. Once I started yelling he grabbed me by my mouth and he started cursing at me. He told me to shut up and if I made any noise or if I kept yelling he would beat me bad. He raped me. It was all a nightmare. When it was over I ran to the bathroom and locked myself in and cried. He banged on the door for me to open it. He yelled if I told anything to my friend or anyone else, he would hurt or kill me if he had to.

When he left I heard the door close. I opened the bathroom door slowly. I was afraid and crying. I wanted to see if he really left. I ran to close the door. I locked the doors. I walked back to the bathroom and sat on the floor, crying, in pain, still in unbelief. I just got raped. I realized I was bleeding. I didn't know what to think since I had never had sex before. I put my clothes on. I looked at myself in the mirror. I had bruises on my face and body. I felt like garbage. I grabbed my bag and left walking. I wasn't going to stay and wait for my friend, what was I going to tell him. Did he know what his friend was up too? I had no idea what to think anymore. I sat under a tree at the park and cried asking why everything bad was always happening to me. I just wanted to get hit by a car and die.

My friend started calling me but I ignored all calls. I didn't know what to do or think anymore. I stayed on the streets from there on. I would call friends and ask if I was able to spend the night at their houses. For days I would hop from house to house. Some people I didn't even know they were just my Myspace friends. There were days where I had nowhere to go. I would walk on the streets all night having no idea what city I was in. Walking all night had to be the worst. I would see people doing drugs, acting weird, and prostitution. I would get stopped all the time and asked if I was interested in working? I just couldn't believe how life was and that the world was cold and people would do anything to make money. I didn't or wasn't interested in money, I just wanted to be in a loving family and live a normal life just like every other thirteen year old.

Sometimes when I didn't have anywhere to spend that day I would get on a bus and stay on it all day until the last stop. One day a bus driver noticed me and asked me where I was going, since I had been on his bus all day and he had noticed I had not gotten off at any of the stops. This was his second time going the same route. I told him I didn't know, and I didn't have much money either, when I was his last stop he gave me twenty dollars and told me to go home. I told him thanks. But I knew for sure I'm not going back home.

Months passed by like that until one day one of my friends called me and told me she had somewhere for me to go. It was her cousin's house in Hollister, Ca. In return for living there they wanted me to watch their kids. Her cousin was a single mother. I was totally fine with that. I would lie about my age. No one had an ideal that I was only thirteen turning fourteen soon. I was picking up and dropping off her kids every day. After a long time I felt like I was in the right place. They didn't treat me like a babysitter. I was like family to them. I lived with them for a whole year and a half.

When I turned fifteen I got caught stealing two candy bars at KMART. I was asked to show ID, and I would be let go, but since I didn't have one, a police officer was called. How was I going to give my real info, I was only fifteen and been missing in the world's eyes for two years already and I didn't want to go back to hell, which was home. Since I told them I was twenty-one they took me to county jail, not juvenile hall, I really didn't know the difference until I arrived there. They needed my fingerprints to find out who I was. I was sat down I was the only person there checking in. I saw men in the holding tank, yelling. I freaked out and started crying, they were about to take my fingerprints and I started shaking and crying. They knew something was wrong, the officers sat me on a bench and asked me what was wrong, and who was I?

The officers were really polite and nice, it seemed like they cared. I was still crying when I told them I was scared because I was in a jail where there's was nobody but crazy old people around me. I told them what my real name was and that I was from the Bay Area. They told me to hold on. I guess they looked up my full name on google and saw I had been missing for two years since I was thirteen years old. They were in shock and you could tell they felt bad for me. They asked me why? How? Two years? The officer quickly took me out of the county jail and took me to the offices where they did foster home locating. I had no idea what that was. The officers let me ride in the passenger seat because he didn't want to handcuff and put me in the back.

On our way there he told me everything was going to be alright. They were looking for a foster home that I could spend the night in since it was really late so I wouldn't have to spend the night in juvie since I didn't commit a major crime. I was taken to a house of an older white woman. She was very nice. She had a bunch of kids already there. They explained to me that I was just going to spend the night there and the next morning they would come get me so they could contact my family. My family? I didn't want to go back there! So I decided once everyone was asleep I would run away from the foster home before they would get there in the morning. I got caught running away. The officers came and I was taken to juvie because they knew that was the only place I wouldn't be able to run from. I was in a cell by myself. It was horrible.

My family was contacted they told my mom to come get me. She came after three days, yes! Three long days. Clearly she didn't care once she arrived. The officer spoke to her, and told her if I ran away because of her again, they would arrest her. And they told me if I were to run away I would be arrested and put in foster care. On my way back home we didn't speak a word. Since I was gone for so long I was required to get a physical check up at the doctors. On the confidential report has a question asking if I have been raped. I put yes. Once I was called in my mom was told to stay out. The doctor checked me did so many tests after she asked me about how it happened. I broke down and told her everything, I didn't like talking much about it because every time it felt like it just happened yesterday, everything would just flashback in my head.

The doctor took me into another room, my mom wanted to know what was going on. They told her to have a seat and wait. I was put in another room where an officer was waiting. I had no idea what was going on. I was wondering what did I do now? I sat down and the officer which was a male wanted to know all the info on the man who hurt and raped me. I started crying because his image would pop in my head every time someone would ask. I knew his name. I told them everything I knew about him. The officer said he was going to see me a couple more times.

My mom was mad. She didn't know what was going on, but she saw the officer so she had an idea. On my way home with my mom she was just yelling at me the whole way home, asking what was I getting into now that I kept ruining their name, blah, blah, blah. She was making me feel like trash. When I had nothing to do with it, I wasn't doing anything wrong. At my visit, I told them I didn't want to continue and wanted to stop everything. I was asked if someone threatened me. I told them no, how was I going to tell them my own mom didn't want me to talk. But God is good. Two weeks later he was arrested for doing the same to another girl. He was on the news. I

still was having problems at home, I got pregnant at age sixteen and my mom kicked me out. I went through it all over again but this time pregnant and kicked out. Not a runaway.

Basically, I never lived a childhood. I ended up living two adult lives. I didn't get to do what other normal kids my age would do. I wish my mom was my best friend, I wish I had someone to talk to. I wish I was born into a different family so that way I would be accepted for who I am and also my kids. Till this day, we are not in contact as well. I'm a hurt soul because I can't forget my past because I lived every minute of it. But I thank God; I never turned to drugs, even when I was offered it a lot of times. Everything has made me a stronger person I am today.

I still have my breaking moments though. I'm telling my story to others, if someone is going through the same situation, don't run away! Get help! I wasn't informed well and I didn't know much back then, but now there's a lot of help out there, something I didn't have. If I can change someone's life by sharing my story, I'm more than happy too. I wouldn't want anyone to go through what I had to in a million years. As a young girl I didn't have anyone to tell me about Jesus. I didn't know about a God who loved me and who was there to heal my broken wounds. I didn't know that there was a better life for me. I wish I had known. I wish by reading my story you will see that you can't find real love in this fallen world. There are broken, hurtful people that will come into your life, but if you have the foundation of Christ to stand on those people will never be able to crush you. I learn the truth of Salvation in Christ many years later. After so many sinful mistakes to actually be free from the heaviness of guilt, shame and pain from my decisions, is real life. You can have it. Jesus wants to be your Savior, let Him. I am currently in jail for crimes that I committed. I have to do this time, no one can do it for me. But I do not feel like a failure. I know God is with me in this place. I am freer now than I have ever been on the streets. This prison is not my identity. My identity is in Christ Jesus. I have a release date from prison, but I am never going to be release from Jesus. And when I get out of here I have a life to live.

Today, I have two little girls, and they are my best friends. I wouldn't change them for anything in the world.

Satan used this young lady's family to knock her down by rejecting and physically abusing her. He then used a man to sexually violate her. She ran away and the abuse continued. She felt so devalued that she made decisions that kept her in bondage and resulted in her criminal behavior. She had given up on herself, on life, and on God.

But thank God He never gave up on her. Thank God she knows He is with her and He loves her to this day. Once you have turn and give your life to Him, He only give you a life worth living.

You want to know how to be successful in this new life? You have to let go of the past, no matter who you are or what has happened to you this is possible.

How can you let go and live? By making the decision to FORGIVE! Holding on to past hurts gives your abusers continual power over you.

By forgiving the offenders and offenses, you stop the enemy (Satan) from having control of your life and your mind. It will stop him from sending you wrong messages, ones like "the attack was your fault, you are ugly and no one will ever love you or you are an addict, and you will always be an addict." These messages will become your new assailants. You will be assaulted over and over again until you let go of the past.

Until you let go of the bondage of guilt and shame, pain and brokenness you will never have freedom. Stop holding onto this bondage like a comfortable blanket that covers you from your reality. You will never live a life of freedom and peace. "Freedom and Peace" these two words are valuable. If you remain in bondage, you will always suffer. No matter what accomplishments you obtain you will always have the voices in your head that tell you that you could have done better. The lies are there because the hurt is still in place. Whatever age you were harmed as that little girl, she is the one who needs the healing.

As a woman, I push and push past the lies, but even for me it came back in other ways. For me it returned in my marriage and my mothering. My husband, who was so supportive of me, never once said these things, but because I came from a background of fear, guilt, shame and people pleasing; I believed the lie of others who observed me from a distant. Their view of me spoke volumes and the words and thoughts that heard over and over was that I was never good enough as a wife or as a mother. I saw myself as a failure, so I got failure messages continually running through my mind. Because of fear of failure, I wore the Masks of perfection and control for so many years. I had to be perfect in everything only to come up short. I had to be in control of everything and everybody, only to be resented for what I thought was showing love. These Masks were heavy and suffocating. I kept them on for a long time until I finally realized I had to give them up or I was going to lose everyone I really loved and needed in my life.

What freedom and peace I found when I gave it all up for Jesus! I am enjoying every day as a new creation in Christ Jesus! It is no longer little Betty (victim), Teddy Bear (fearful), or just Betty (people pleaser). I am no longer scared to live or love, I am no longer controlled by the power of someone else and I no longer see myself as having to control everything or be controlled by anyone. I am living a life of abundant joy, peace and prosperity in Christ Jesus.

I don't have to put on airs for anyone. I don't have to worry if I will fit in with this group or with that girl. I don't have to worry if old "friends" will reject me after reading this book or even if they will read this book. I do not worry about what I cannot control. This is my truth, my deliverance and I am holding onto it. I am free! This same freedom is for you too. Again, it starts out with the first decision of accepting Jesus as your Lord and Savior. And then ask Jesus to help you let go of the past hurts and to help you forgive those who caused those hurts. Give ALL of it to Jesus.

STRATEGY 5: DECISION OR DENIAL

As I prepared to write Strategy 5, I listened to this song that really spoke to me about the subject of wearing a mask, performing for others and about my giving up on having my rebellious life. Read a few lyrics of the song and see if you agree. Losing My Religion, by Lauren Daigle (song) [19]

> *I've been an actor on a stage*
> *Playin' a role I have to play I'm getting' tired, it's safe to say*
> *Livin' behind a masquerade... (My, my, my)*
> *No more performin' out of fear*
> *I'm tryin' to keep my conscience clear*
> *It all seemed so insincere*
> *I'd trade it all to meet You here... (My, my, my)*
> *I'm losing my religion... (My, my, my)*
> *Light a match and watch it burn*
> *And to Your heart I will return*
> *No one can love me like You do*
> *Oh no, no, no, no*
> *So why would I want a substitute?*
> *I'm losing my religion*
> *To find you*
> *(My, my, my)*

This strategy is written for those of you who are performing, be it as a youth growing up in the church, on the system or is currently incarcerated. It does not matter what walk of life you come from you still have to come to this point of deciding for yourself. Decision or Denial? As the song reveals, it's time for you to have a real relationship with the One who gives true life and security. He is the One who brings restoration to your life. He is the One who heals you and make you whole. His name is Jesus Christ. I have introduced Him to you earlier. I have spoken about Him continuously in the book.

For so many years, I had lived a religious life. I started out as a youth in a church on an island in Georgia. I joined the youth choir. We traveled to different cities and performed. I was in a relationship with the assistant choir director. I would travel anywhere as long as I was with him. I was also with my best friend, his sister. I spoke of them both in this earlier writing. I played whatever role I had to just to fit in with them. I loved (well what I thought was love), him so much. I learned how to be a loving, committed girlfriend.

The Mask I wore here was the fear of being exposed and the fear of being rejected by him. So, I was living a fearful life while dating him. I was so afraid that one day he was going to drop me like a bad habit. Well you guessed it, that day came, and I wanted to die! I was devastated. I couldn't believe it when he called me on the phone. Yes, ladies the phone, coward, to say he wanted us to be just friends. He said he just needed space to work on his music. He wanted to know if we could be friends. But of course, by the next rehearsal he was already working toward his relationship with the next girl in the group with his sister's help. I was lost and I didn't know how to fit in with the group because I lost what I thought was my identity. My identity was in him as his girlfriend. I was serving the wrong god.

The reality was I didn't know who my True Lover was. I didn't know Jesus. In the choir we sang songs using His name. Some people shouted, jumped around and past out under His Spirit.

I mimicked some of their actions just to appear saved. I didn't even know how to seek Him (Jesus). I just found a place in the church world to hide. I wasn't in church to learn and grow in Christ. I didn't even know how to reach Him. He was just an idea to obtain, but a reality to me that I wasn't good enough to know. They didn't really teach the youth about Christ's love for them at that time. You sat in church with the adults and listened to the preacher preach. The Amen and Hallelujahs ring out from the deacon and usher board. I never got the messages because I never really listen.

I was there for hanging out with my friends. We didn't have youth studies or groups like they have in some churches today. That was my teen years. Let me tell you I was so lost not knowing who I was in Christ that for many years later I was still performing. Claiming to be a Christian was just another mask that I wore. It was one of the most condemning masks of all. I thought being a Christian was a lot of rules, and do's and don'ts, a perfect holier than most righteous person. All I can see is this ugliness, unwanted and unclean girl. No Jesus will ever want me.

Years later I served in a local church in California for fifteen years. I was the youth director for the church for eight of those years and then an ordained elder until I left. I was very active with the youth and women's ministry. I was very active in the church. I served with the hospitality, elder board and counseling ministry. I can tell you to this day how to run a church program. I can tell you how to serve a pastor/bishop and other visiting ministers like they were kings. I found myself serving and worshipping man GREATER than serving and worshipping the LORD. I had the church serving down. But if you ask me about my relationship with the Lord, I couldn't say much. I didn't study His Word or spend time with Him in prayer. I didn't open His Word for myself. I just sat and got preached to. Now I was the one saying the Amen, Hallelujahs and preach pastor! I had been well trained by the adult usher board and, I imitated the same behavior that I despised. Jesus was the titled Name I heard about. But He was not who I sought to know for myself. The funny thing is I taught Him to the youth, and I did learn of Him, but I was not hungry to know Him fully. My spiritual life was dry and lifeless. I was serving the other idol gods, man, distractions and self.

The Word of God tells that our Lord is a jealous God and He will not share us with anything or anyone outside of Himself. Wow someone loves me so much not to share me. Read the below Scriptures and it tells you just how serious our Lord is. In Exodus 20:1-5 (NKJV) says:

> *"I am the LORD your God, who brought you out of the land of Egypt (Hell), out of the house of bondage (shame, guilt and pain). "You shall have no other gods before Me. "You shall not make for yourself a carved image—any likeness of anything that is in heaven above, or that is in the earth beneath, or that is in the water under the earth; you shall not bow*

down to them nor serve them. For I, the LORD your God, am a jealous God, visiting the iniquity of the fathers upon the children to the third and fourth generations of those who hate Me."

This is what I am finding in many churches today. People are serving the heads (all the titles of leadership) of the churches and forgetting to serve with their whole hearts the True Head of the Church, Jesus Christ. I recognize it as a "need to be needed, look at me" type personality. This type of person is one who seeks out the approval and praises from everyone. They need to hear what a great job they are doing. And when the praises don't come their heart and feelings gets hurt because no one approved or praised them. This is not only in the churches. It is in the schools, workplaces and homes etc. This is one example of fake "righteous" living that is happening. Like the song says, "Actors on the stage of performing arts."

This chapter is not about the fake living in the church or anywhere else. I write it to bring light into a dark area of living for our young people today. What I see in our young people is they either want nothing to do with church or any organized religion. Some who are performing in the church and are currently in the church building, are living an inactive Christian life. They come to church because they are required to by their parent(s). If they don't come, they are made to feel guilty. Their hearts are so far from God because they are looking at themselves and everything and everyone as fake performers. Young person these thoughts are stumbling blocks in your way to keep you from truly knowing who you are and who you belong to. The Word of God does tell us in Romans 16:17-20 (AMP)

> *"I urge you, brothers and sisters, to keep your eyes on those who cause dissensions (disagreements) and create obstacles or introduce temptations [for others] to commit sin, [acting in ways] contrary to the doctrine which you have learned. Turn away from them. For such people do not serve our Lord Christ, but their own appetites and base (corrupt) desires. By smooth and flattering speech they deceive the hearts of the unsuspecting [the innocent and the naive]. For the report of your obedience has reached everyone, so that I rejoice over you, but I want you to be wise in what is good and innocent in what is evil. The God of peace will soon crush Satan under your feet. The [wonderful] grace of our Lord Jesus be with you."*

These Scriptures tells you that you are indeed to keep your eyes open to those things and people that cause you to think and desire any temptations that are an obstacle to your knowing and growing in a relationship with Jesus. You must understand that you have an enemy and he wants to take you out of the game of life. Satan is your tempter and the liar. He uses people and teachings to deceive your heart and mind.

As I looked at some of the young girls at my church the Lord spoke to my heart and allowed me to speak to them openly about their relationship with God, parents, schools and friends. My heart ached from their truth that was shared with me. As I share their truths I ask you to look and see if you recognize yourself in any part of their stories. The young girls whom I have talked with are living a two-sided life. Their masks look something like this:

- At home, school and church I am a respectful helper. I am quiet until I am asked a question. No one knows me really, not even my parents. I hate my life and I hate them. No one sees me. I am always nervous, full of anxieties and depression. No one can ever know how I feel, or what I am thinking. So I must keep on my Masks or the real me will be exposed! I am invisible.
- At home, school and church (when I go) I am distant. I am rebellious and I hate being there and they hate me. I am disrespectful to any authority, especially my parents. They fight with me to go to church. To me they are all a bunch of hypocrites. I don't believe in their God or any God. To me, He isn't real. He is just a bunch of religious talk. They want me to be this perfect girl. But how can I ever be, when all I am ever told is that I should act more like this or more like her. What is wrong with me, why can't I just… this tells me that the real me is not lovable or good enough, so I don't respond in love…I am invisible.. ?
- At home I am very demanding of my mom. It's because of her I don't have my dad. I am not happy with her or him. I am angry all the time. I demand things from her that I know we can't afford. Sometimes I get it and sometimes I don't. I only text my dad when I want something from him, mostly money. We don't have that father/daughter relationship you find in the movies. No, our relationship is weak to say the

least. My mom and grandparents took me to church when I was younger. The church we sometimes go to is so boring. There is nothing there for teens. The pastor is demeaning at times to the three or four teens that still come. He banned us from bringing cellphones inside the church. The adults can still use theirs but we can't even bring them out of the car. Truth be told I was just looking at my pictures or using up our limited data and not listening to him. If only adults would understand church got to be entertaining or no young person would want to be there. Most of the time I am tired and I just want to stay home. Sometimes I am bugged into going though. If only my mom knew the truth about how I feel about God. Here it is. He's alright. I ain't got no problem with Him. He's just alright. No one knows the real me...I am invisible.

One girl is fearful of living. She is afraid to breathe or use her voice to speak up and be heard. The other girl is fighting against everyone and everything. She believes the lies that have been told to her that she is not good enough. If she keeps everyone away, then she can't be rejected or hurt by anyone again. The last girl is hurt and broken from the divorce of her parents. She has not been given a voice in the divorce. So, she reacts in a hurtful behavior. This way she won't get hurt by anyone else if she keeps everyone at bay.

Neither girl knows how to express their fears, hurt and anger in a healthy way. Neither one has been introduced to Jesus as their Savior, Lord, Lover and Hope. They are feeling unlovable, unwanted and is rebelling. The feelings of being not good enough comes from the lies of the enemy, Satan. He has blinded them in fear and fight. He has a hold on their hearts that can only be taken back by the Power of Jesus Christ.

If you find yourself somewhere in between the three Masked girls. Ask yourself, especially if you are currently a girl who has been or is being a victim of a predator and you can only see the ugly in your life. Ask yourself if you are strong enough and ready to make the Decision to L.I.V.E.

I want you to read the lyrics of this song and see if you can find it in yourself to turn this song into a prayer: Rebel heart Lauren Daigle (Song) [20]

Lord, I offer up this rebel heart

So stubborn and so restless from the start
I don't wanna fight You anymore
So take this rebel heart and make it Yours
Father, I no longer want to run
You've broken my resistance with Your love
And drowned it underneath the crimson spill
So bend this rebel heart to
Your will I give it over to You,
I give it over to You
Your love is like an arrow, straight and true
And now this rebel hearts belongs to You
Help me lay the renegade to rest
Turn the stone inside me back to flesh
And hold me till my best defenses fall
And watch this rebel heart surrender all
I give it over to You, I give over to You
Your love is like an arrow, straight and true
And now this rebel heart belongs to You
Oh, take my life and let it be Yours
I give it over to You, I give it over to You
Your love is like an arrow, straight and true
And now this rebel heart belongs to You
Now this rebel heart belongs to You
In Jesus's name Amen!

Wow! This song is truly a prayer for you, who is tired of running and who is longing to live a life of freedom and wholeness. Freedom from the bondage of guilt, shame and pain from your past is true living. It's time to STAND up and use Your voice. TAKE back Your Power to say NO! NO MORE! OWN Your own story. Rewrite Your new beginning and PROTECT Your God given rights to L.I.V.E.

It is time to make the decision to live a Mask free life. A life that can be dedicated to worshipping and serving One Master, One Savior and One Lord. The True Living God. One who is Life and Light.

Basically we are not free to ourselves. Outward situations are not in our hands, they are in God's hands. The one thing in which we have freedom in is how personal we allow God into a relationship with us. We are not responsible for the circumstances we are in, but we are responsible for the way we allow those circumstances to affect us. We can either allow them to keep us in bondage or we can allow the trajectory of our lives to change into what God wants us to be.

Or maybe you have made the decision to continue to live a life in bondage to your past. Bondage to the control of what others want from you and think of you. Their thoughts and demands only keeps you in the bondage of fear, anxiety, depression and regrets. These bondages keep you in a life dictated by the evil gods. The gods of your past hurts, gods your family ties, gods of unsafe friends and enemies, gods of addictions to drugs, alcohol and sexual promiscuity, all the gods of a failed life. How about bowing down to the gods of self, or the gods of lies and defeat. The gods of fear or the gods of depression, oppression and anxiety.

This decision comes from accepting life as it is instead of life as it can be in Christ Jesus. In this current life you have been defeated! If you still have some confusion as to what decision you should make, read the scriptures below and allow them to speak into your decision. Read and think on them and then ask yourself, "Who this day will I serve?" Joshua 24:14-24 The Message (MSG) "So now: Fear God. Worship him in total commitment. Get rid of the gods your ancestors worshiped on the far side of The River (the Euphrates) and in Egypt. You, worship God.

> *"If you decide that it's a bad thing to worship God, then choose a god you'd rather serve—and do it today. Choose one of the gods your ancestors worshiped from the country beyond The River, or one of the gods of the Amorites, on whose land you're now living. As for me and my family, we'll worship God." The people answered, "We'd never forsake God! Never! We'd never leave God to worship other gods. "God is our God! He brought up our ancestors from Egypt and from slave conditions. He did all those great signs while we watched. He has kept his eye on us all along the roads we've traveled and among the nations we've passed through. Just for us he drove out all the nations, Amorites and all, who lived in the land. "Count us in: We too are going to worship God. He's our God." 19-20*
>
> *Then Joshua told the people: "You can't do it; you're not able to worship God. He is a holy God. He is a jealous God. He won't put up with your fooling around and sinning. When you leave God and take up the worship of foreign gods, he'll turn right around and come down on you hard. He'll put an end to you—and after all the good he has done for you!" 21 But the people told Joshua: "No! No! We worship God!" 22*
>
> *And so Joshua addressed the people: "You are witnesses against yourselves that you have chosen God for yourselves—to worship him." And they said, "We are witnesses." 23 Joshua said, "Now get rid of all the foreign gods you have with you. Say an unqualified Yes to God, the God of Israel." 24 The people answered Joshua, "We will worship God. What he says, we'll do."*

A declaration I live by: AS FOR ME AND MY HOUSE WE SHALL SERVE THE LORD. *(Joshua 24:15-20, 22-24 MSG)*

God's promises never fail. After God had given Israel all the land He had promised, He also gave them "rest." And amazingly, "not one of the good promises which the Lord had spoken to the house of Israel failed; all had come to pass" (Joshua 21:45).

According to Romans 15:13, "we can be filled with all joy and peace in believing" not doubting or being negative, but by believing. Romans 15:13 New Living Translation (NLT) says, "I pray that God, the source of hope, will fill you completely with joy and peace because you trust in him. Then you will overflow with confident hope through the power of the Holy Spirit." We all believe something but believing only God's Word produces the results whereby we may "abound in hope and overflow with confidence in His promises." Think about this, by just being positive, having the best perspectives on everything, and always believing the best of everybody, we release peace and joy in our lives. We get what we believe, what we think, and what we meditate on, so believe God's Word and expect peace and joy.

These Scriptures tell you that if you choose to live a life devoted to Christ, that you are also to believe the promises He gave to the Israelites are the same promises that He gives you today. Just as He gave me the ministry of God's Awesome Promises. I can say without a doubt He has and is carrying out every promise He has for me. My life devoted to Him is strong and His faithfulness to me is even stronger. I am excited about serving Him. I have great zeal and passion in my pursuit of Him. It is a great thing to be excited, devoted and passionate these are all positive emotions. They give us fire in our spirit and liveliness in our bones to make us press forward in our pursuit of a better life. The Bible instructs us to be zealous and enthusiastic as we serve the Lord.

What are you enthusiastically pursuing?

Who do you choose to serve this day?

What are the promises you are believing for yourself today?

"Never be lazy but work hard and serve the Lord enthusiastically" Romans 12:11 (NLT).

We are to serve the Lord with all that we are. I made the decision that I wanted to serve God only and in doing so immediately I saw myself as a big water pitcher. It was filled with a dirty, cloudy, watery substance to the very top. This dirty pitcher represented how I saw myself. The Lord called me to Himself. He said to me (Betty) come to me (Him) and when you come, come as you are. I didn't have to dress up all pretty or be proper and start saying the right words or work hard to get His approval. All I had to do is go to Him and give my all to Him. What does it mean to give your all? Well it's a daily process. This process doesn't start until you first accept Jesus Christ as you Lord and Savior. Romans 10:10 (AMP) says, "For with the heart a person believes (adheres to, trust in, and relies on Christ) and so is justified (declared righteous, acceptable to God), and with the mouth he confesses (declares openly and speaks out freely his faith) and confirms (his) salvation." That's step one to your new beginning. The process continues as you allow the Holy Spirit (God's own working power) to work through you daily. To surrender to a force that is greater than you is so freeing and life changing. And that's step two to your new deliverance. And finally step three, believing by faith you have received both salvation and deliverance from God is your sanctification. Believe you have been set apart for God's own creative use is the new you. As for me, as I poured out my filthy substance before the Lord, I asked God to accept my offering and to cleanse me of the filth and to fill me with all He has for me. And I asked Him to help me receive Him totally. I didn't just want to be an empty pitcher or a pretty pitcher that was sitting on a shelf not being used. I wanted to be one that was full and useful to God. He had chosen me and now I want to be used by Him.

That is why I love the book of Isaiah. In chapter 6 it talks about the call of God and those who have answered His call. In

Isaiah 6:8 (AMP) the Prophet heard the voice of the Lord, saying: "Whom shall I send, and who will go for Us?" Then I said, "Here am I; send me".

I believe I was called by the Lord. This doesn't make me something special. The Word of God says the call of God is not for a selected few but for everyone. But everyone has to have the ear to hear Him. I learned that you can't just have ears to hear, you must also have the right condition of the ears and heart to hear from Him. You must also have the right spiritual attitude.

Many are called, but few are chosen (Matthew 22: 14). The chosen ones are those who have come into a relationship with God through Jesus Christ and have had their spiritual condition changed and their ears open. God does not force His will on us. I want you to remove that thought from your mind that God is going to force you or plead with you to come to Him. Just as Jesus called his disciples, He did it with a quiet "follow Me". His call to me was gentle and I until my ears and heart was right I didn't hear Him. He never stopped gently calling me though. When I got hungry for Him, meaning I was tired of living in a multitude of fear, I called out for Him and this is when I heard Him clearly. In Matthew 4:19 Jesus said to His disciples, "Follow Me" (as My disciples, accepting Me as your Master and Teacher and walk the same path of life that I walk) and I will make you fishers of men.

In Joshua 22:5 (ESV) says, "We are to love the Lord our God and walk in His ways and keep His commandments and hold fast to Him and serve Him with all your heart and with all your soul (with everything you are and everything you have)."

Why should we do this? Simply because God expects us to trust that everything He does is for our ultimate good.

Good emotions come from good decisions and good thoughts. One way to enjoy a joyful life in Christ is expect good things to happen for you. You cannot wake up every day with the attitude that says I am going to get up and wait to see how I feel and I am going to let those feelings dictate the course of my day. I say Instead of waking up with that mindset, wake up strong and empowered by the Holy Spirit and ask Him to help you set your mind in the right direction ahead of time before putting your feet on the floor. He will lead you in making the decisions that will produce right emotions that will help you enjoy your day.

After reading this story about Professor Bi I wanted to share it with you. His story gives you a great example of how big our God is and how His Son Jesus keeps His promises of being with you always. No matter where you are, Jesus is with you. No matter how low of a pit you find yourself in, He will pull you out of that pit, place you safely and securely in His arms like He did for this professor in the story.

This story is shared to all but especially for you young person that currently finds yourself in jail or locked in a prison cell or trapped in a slave or sex trafficking. You feel you are locked away and is in a desperate situation. You may find yourselves in a mindset like Mr. Bi and you see no way out of your miserable condition but to cause harm to yourself. I ask you to read this story and see how Jesus spoke in His small reassuring voice, "Don't go. Don't go!" I say to you Don't give up and Don't give in to the call of death. Read this story and I say to you test God in this, see if your true redemption (rescue) will come.

A young man named Ryan shares a story of a man named Mr. Bi who was a professor at Beijing University, known as "the Harvard of China." He made a joke in class about the Communist party to a group of students. One of those students reported his joke to the police. The next day officers burst into Mr. Bi's office and brought him to a remote, cold Communist prison—without warning and without a trial.

He woke up that morning as a professor chairing one of the most prestigious academic positions in the world. By nightfall, he was behind bars in prison. Chinese prisons at this time were some of the worst places on earth—horrible lairs of disease, torture and death. Mr. Bi quickly plunged into depression and despair. His depression led to thoughts of suicide over the course of weeks. One afternoon, in a cloud of sadness, he brought himself to the window of his eighth-story prison cell. The Chinese did not put windows in the higher floors of prison cells. If a prisoner decided to throw himself to his death, it was not a problem.

Mr. Bi's heart raced as he looked out and thought of jumping. And then it happened. He heard a small voice say, "Don't go. Don't go. Don't go." He sat down in the middle of his cell, desperate.

There on the hard-concrete floor, memories flooded his mind. A friend of his, a foreign professor who was a Christian, had shared the Gospel with him. Mr. Bi prayed, "Jesus, if You are real, please bring me this forgiveness and peace my friend told me You promised. In turn, I will offer my life and service to You."

He looked up and, "The sky was never bluer. The sun was never brighter through the open hole of a window and I had joy rise up inside of my heart like I have never felt before."

> *This distinguished professor threw all his reservations away and shouted out, "I have a bright future in Jesus Christ!" The guards heard him and cruelly told him to be quiet. But his joy could not be contained. He kept shouting it over and over until they came into the cell and beat him.*
>
> *A person in a prison freed by believing the Gospel of Jesus is freer than any person outside of prison without the Gospel.*

Mr. Bi was eventually released. He did not become bitter because of his treatment, instead he allowed his prison experience to serve others for God. He started several orphanages in the interior of China, caring for the poor and leading many to Christ. He had a bright future in Jesus Christ. To this day his joy is infectious when you meet him. And he will tell you the joy he had in prison is the same he has to this day.

Every person feels at times they are in a prison of their own making—trapped by thoughts, habits, actions, and a nagging past that will not let them go.

The Gospel teaches us that the worst of all prisons are the ones we make for ourselves. The cells of this prison are barred with our insecurities, with the deep awareness that something is not right inside us and that something is deeply broken. We carry this with us like chains around our necks. It is the human condition of brokenness.

This will only change if something drastic happens. The Gospel is the most drastic of measures. It's a bloody cross that Jesus Himself endured on our behalf. It's the death of God Himself for our sins. It's the utter smashing defeat of death itself and the hold that death had on us, in a glorious resurrection of Christ Jesus, to show God's love and power throughout all eternity.

Scripture reminds us that we must pay close attention to what we have heard, especially when it comes to the Gospel. Hebrews 2:1 (MSG),

> *"It is crucial that we keep a firm grip on what we've heard so that we don't drift off. If the old message delivered by the angels was valid and nobody got away with anything, do you think we can risk neglecting this latest message, this magnificent salvation? First of all, it was delivered in person by the Master, then accurately passed on to us by those who heard it from Him. All the while God was validating it with gifts through the Holy Spirit, all sorts of signs and miracles, as He saw fit."*

Scripture continues to say, in Romans 8:37-39 (MSG),

> *"No, in all these things we are more than conquerors through Him who loved us. For I am sure that neither death nor life, nor angels nor rulers, nor things to come, nor powers, nor heights nor death, nor anything else in all creation, will be able to separate us from the love of God in Christ Jesus our Lord."*

He took our rightful punishment upon Himself. So that today, even on your loneliest days, you'll never lack for relationships in your life, both with God and with man.

Jesus paid with His life for you to always have Him close to you. Don't believe for one moment that you're meant to live a lonely life. In Christ Jesus you are never alone, and you are always cared for. In Hebrews 13:5 (TPT),

> *"(God) Himself has said, don't be obsessed with money but live content with what you have, you always have God's presence. For hasn't He promised you, "I will never leave you alone, never! And I will not loosen my grip on your life!" so we can say with confidence: "I know the Lord is for me and I will never be afraid of what people may do to me!"*

The most important sermon you will ever preach is the one you preach to yourself. Getting God's Word in your own heart, daily reminding you of His truth and promises for you will give you the power to stand against all that will come after you. You are not alone in this fight! God Himself in fighting for you. You have got to release the battle to the Lord and not try and take back the fight and the control. It's not easy but it is very much so worth it. It's having faith that God is bigger than any battle you have and to believe with your heart that He is Lord. Change comes with your having faith in God that as you change the words that you speak or allow others to speak in your heart, by erasing the recordings that repeated the old failure messages. Record a new message, one like, "I have a bright future in Jesus Christ, I am never alone!

God has a purpose and plan for me. I am valuable to God Almighty! He knows my name, and He is calling me to Himself daily, because He loves me!" This is how you fight against the mental powers of darkness and be freed from that same darkness. Don't think Satan is going to lay down and give up trying to control you, oh No! But before going on let me assure you that he can't win unless you give him the power to. He is as insignificant as you want him to be. I just want to make sure you know he is still in the fight until Jesus Himself comes back to get us.

So, in this new freedom you now have in Jesus, you must remember to always, as best as you can anyway, remain in His presence. What does it mean to remain in His presence? Allow the Holy Spirit, who is now dwelling in you to fill you with the desire of a love relationship for the presence of Jesus. There is no substitution for His presence in your life. You don't have to look for love, you have it in Him.

There are going to be a lot of distractions that are going to come to stop you from having this personal intimate relationship with Jesus. The enemy is going to still come after you and try to tempt you with the thoughts that you need to have certain people, places and things in your life to make you special and complete. These distractions cannot take the place of Jesus. They just can't. They will cause you great pain and disappointment when you try to substitute them for Christ. They will fail you.

There are other distractions from you old life that will come and you will have to face them down with the help of the Holy Spirit. Distractions like old habits, especially the ones that are addictive in nature, will try to retake your life. All distractions are not as destructive as harmful addictions, you can be simply distracted by things such as T.V. shows binge watching, overindulging in food, social media, work, school perfectionism.

We can go on and on but what I am simple saying is that our distractions tend to replace our intimate time with the Father, who has the desire, ability, power to search our hearts, help us face our pain and fears and be healed. We have to stop trying to mask our pain and fears with any distractions. God has us and He has empowered and equipped us with the ability to stand against the distractions. Don't think I am not talking to myself. I have to constantly be reminded to fight against all the distractions that bombards my mind daily. It will always be a choice that you will have to make.

Choose to be with Him, dwell with Him and He will dwell with you, seek Him first and He will supply your every need. He not Santa Claus, or a magical genie, or a magician, no He is not any of those things. These things are fake, man-made, and powerless. God is not powerless, He is God, our Creator, All Powerful, and All-Knowing, God!

My heart was always burdened with sin-consciousness and condemnation. One day, I heard a preacher on television speak on righteousness and my identity in Christ. The understanding that I received from his simple explanation truly transformed my life. By listening to his sermons and that from other teachers and preacher of God's Word, this helped me to finally realize that Jesus loves me just as I am. I do not have to prove my worthiness to Him because He has made me worthy. I no longer suffer from depression, panic attacks, anxiety and suicidal or fearful thoughts. I feel so FREE in this phase of my life because of His grace and faithfulness toward me. All through the Word of God, the promises and rewards I have received come from my reading and hearing it. His Word has set this project girl FREE!

THE REASON FOR MY HOPE

When we look at the undesired situations in our lives. We will find ourselves standing at the threshold of either falling into the pains of despair or falling into the arms of a gracious, loving and caring God—a God who wants to carry us over that painful despair into a wide-open spacious place of hope. There is hope in Christ Jesus.

Now I have given you my best reasoning for my decision for choosing Christ. I have shared stories of other girls who have suffered from similar abuse like you and I, young women who were prisoners of their life choices. Young broken girls who themselves came to the end of their rope and realized they too had to make a decision. Not everyone chose Christ. Ones like Shae Shae who is still looking for her abusers to apologize or make payments to her for hurting her. She is looking for redemption in the wrong savior. But in the end, the choice is up to you. So now I ask you, is it enough for you to make your decision? Do you want to live free or remain in a life of bondage? You choose? But know this, God will never give up on you and neither will I. You must have Hope.

Hope defined is a feeling of expectation and desire for a certain thing to happen. It's more than a wish for change, but an expectation for change. The hope that I am sharing with you is a hope that you can believe in, and you can have a strong feeling toward the change that is to come into your life, and with this hope you can have confidence in the God of Hope. He doesn't deny the reality of our pain, but He does give us a life beyond our pain. He gives us permission for a new beginning. His hope is the happy and confident expectation of good that lifts our spirits and dares us to believe for a different future. Hope is always looking to God: "And now, Lord, what do I wait for and expect? My hope and expectation are in you" Psalm 39:7 (AMP).

We only can do what we are able to do in our own strength until we become worn out from trying. But when we learn to trust and lean into God, when we run to our stronghold Jesus, He promises to overflow our lives with hope: "May the God of your hope fill you with all joy and peace in believing (through experience of your faith) as you trust in Him, so that by the power of the Holy Spirit you may abound and be overflowing (bubbling over) with hope." Romans 15:13 (AMP). He promises to help us become the prisoners of hope He has called us to be so we can stay hopeful, free to step into a new beginning that we might have never visualized.

Sometimes I think hope is an act of defiance, one that God wants us to boldly commit. It's daring to believe in spite of our losses, or abuse and in spite of our disappointments. It's refusing to throw away our confidence and trusting God to reward us because we don't. It's daring not to give up, and when others say, "don't get your hopes up," that is exactly what we do again and again and again!

When we risk hoping again, we learn how to L.I.V.E. in the present with our future in mind. We move our focus forward. We become prisoners of hope who cling to hope, who speak the language of hope, who don't put off hope, who live in a place of freedom letting God surprise in our new beginning. When we become prisoners of hope, then hope quits being on hold, and the desires God placed in our hearts will be fulfilled— somehow and some way.

If you are willing to allow the Holy Spirit to bring you into a personal relationship with the Heavenly Father, our Lord and God, you too will hear what , The Prophet Isaiah and many others before have heard "the voice of Him (God) who is calling you". You too can hear our Savior and Lord's voice. In perfect freedom you too will answer His call with a strong Yes! Here I am Lord send me. Send me!

STRATEGY 6: THE CELEBRATION

As I prepared to write this chapter, I shared with my best friend and closest sister that I was currently struggling with explaining the celebration process to my readers. She asked me a question that really made me stop and think.

She asked me "Betty, have you ever celebrated your victories? If so, how? If not, why not?". I paused before answering because truth be told, I have never rejoiced over my victories. I had never celebrated the breakthroughs and healing process of my life's journey. I have always given glory and praise to the Lord for my victories, which is what we are to do, and in doing so I took the glory off of me. But I was still hiding in fear of being exposed. Afraid of the victories I quietly lived behind another mask. So, as I sit here pondering what this means to celebrate and what it looks like. I asked the Holy Spirit to show me what my victories look like and here is what He showed me:

Celebrating your victories is a process. The way I look at my victory in this journey is like this: the enemy (Satan) had plans to take me out when I was young, through the abuse, but the Lord said "No!" The enemy tried to make me what he wanted me to be. But the Lord had a new identity for me. As a teenager, I wanted to end my life because of the pain, shame and guilt that came from the abuse. But again, the Lord said, "No!" Today, I can stand confidently knowing what it means to celebrate because I overcame the enemy! Through the power of the Holy Spirit I snapped the neck of that old devil.

As I look at this little project girl's life, I can see deep sadness from all the pain I suffered. Satan wants me to dwell on this sadness, but I refuse to. I made a choice not to dwell in the past. The Lord gave me a new life. In this life, He gave me great liberty.

My Heavenly Father saved me from a life of destruction because I learned to put my total trust in Him. Many of my family members and friends made wrong choices as a result of their abuse. As you read from the stories in this book, many other women made the same mistakes. But our Gracious God did not leave them there. That is why I say to you your past life doesn't have to be your story just like it isn't mine. I celebrate because throughout my teenage years, and the many bad decisions that I have made, the Lord forgave me of my sins. Through His mercy and grace, He helped me to forgive myself.

I celebrate because I know I have been healed in so many areas of my life. Every door that I allow the Lord to open, although it may hurt, that little discomfort outweighs the benefit of the healing. There are still many areas to go, but the fears that used to control my heart and life has been defeated. This does not mean I do not fear at times. But it does mean I push forward and do whatever I have to do despite the fear. Because I no longer own fear, and the fear no longer owns me.

I celebrate because I look at how the Lord brought an awesome man, my husband, into my life that has helped in this healing process. My husband is not my healer or my lord, but he my very best friend and my love.

I celebrate because the Lord did not hold the sin of abortion against me. He forgave me and blessed us with an incredible son, whom I love deeply and dearly. He and his wife, my daughter–in–love, have blessed us with five beautiful grandchildren. In them I see the hand of God and the many blessings He gives me daily.

I celebrate because I graduated from high school, went to college and joined the United States Navy.

I celebrate because I look at my law enforcement career of over thirty years of service and realize that it was by the grace of God that I was able to serve. I celebrate because I can! I celebrate because I am alive! I am not dead! I celebrate because of what the enemy meant for my harm, God turned around for my good.

You, too, can celebrate. Take some time to write your declarations.

I celebrate because ...

Not only can you celebrate what you have accomplished, but you can create a future that is bright. A future hoped for one that is still being written. It starts by writing down your vision.

Who do you see?

What about your life do you like?

What about your life do you want to change?

What does your tomorrow look like?

What does five years from now look like?

What does ten years from now look like?

Let your heart and mind be opened to your future. Ask the Holy Spirit to help you visualize your future and your promises. You are in control of what you do. If you are currently being victimized, you can do something about it today! And you are not and never will be alone. The Bible teaches us "To be strong and that no man can take away from you. No one can steal it, kill it or destroy it. God has your promises.

Celebrate now because you have the victory over your past and the power to triumph in your present circumstances. Victory first comes through forgiveness. We are to forgive others and we ourselves will be forgiven. Despite all the things you have gone through, this is the promise of our Lord and Savior: that overwhelming victory is yours through Christ, who loves you. God intends to restore everything that was stolen from you.

Celebrate because you have chosen to live a life of forgiveness, although not easy, but well worth it. Take a moment to learn more about the power of forgiveness and how this relates to the celebration process.

HEALING PAST WOUNDS AND FORGIVING PRESENT SCARS

> *"He himself bore our sins in His body on the tree, that we might die to sin and live to righteousness. By His wounds you have been healed"* 1 Peter 2:24 (AMP)

All of us have experienced trial and pain. You might not be a victim of sexual or physical, you might be struggling with mental abuse from someone that was supposed to care for you. It doesn't matter what your experience was it is safe to say, we are all living with wounds and scars of some kind.

One of the most important, spiritual exercises we can undergo is allowing God to heal our past wounds and guide us to a lifestyle of forgiving present scars. Without healing and forgiveness, other people's mistakes will affect our future. They will still have control over our future. Our new written stories. Without the inner workings of the Holy Spirit, we will live in continual suffering from the sins of others.

Our God is a God of healing. Psalm 147:3 (NKJV) says, "He heals the brokenhearted and binds up their wounds." Psalm 103:2-5 (MSG) says, "O my soul, bless GOD. From head to toe, I'll bless His holy name! O my soul, bless GOD, don't forget a single blessing! He forgives your sins – everyone. He heals your diseases – every one. He redeems you from hell – saves your life! He crowns you with love and mercy – a paradise crown. He wraps you in goodness – beauty eternal. He renews your youth (like a soaring eagle)– you're always young in his presence." 1 Peter 2:24 (NLT) says, "He himself bore our sins in his body on the tree, that we might die to sin and live to righteousness. By his wounds you have been healed." Our heavenly Father longs to speak to the wounded places in our life and to heal them with His love.

What past experience, trial, hurtful words, or person is still harmfully affecting your life today? Name them or it don't be afraid, be free! Where do you need the Holy Spirit to come and speak healing over you? What doors are you willing to open and allow God to bring healing to restore you there? Where do you need to cry out to God in anger or frustration over a wound? Do you believe He is All-Powerful God who can take whatever hurt your throw at Him? Opening the wounded places of our hearts is an emotional and difficult process. But until we allow God in to heal us, we will never experience true freedom and restoration.

This opens the door to forgiveness. We must forgive those who hurt us so the scars in our lives become symbols of God's redeeming love rather than reminders of painful events. James 2:13 (NLT) says, "There will be no mercy for those who have not shown mercy to others. But if you have been merciful, God will be merciful when He judges you." Show mercy to those who are undeserving of it just as your heavenly Father has shown you mercy. Love your enemies as Jesus did (not for their benefit but for your own) so that you can experience triumph instead of pain, freedom instead of bondage to negativity, and joy instead of anger. May your heavenly Father be allowed to love you, hold you and care for the places in your heart that needs His healing touch.

I want to share a few stories with you about some women who were enslaved and sexually assaulted. It's not the trauma of their stories that are most compelling but rather how they opened themselves to forgiveness and to see how the power of forgiveness opened doors of freedom for their lives. I can see the hand of God on their lives throughout their stories, can you?

KARLA'S STORY

Karla's story will ring true for a lot of us who were victimized at a very young age. I share her story because it is one of victory. Karla was lured from poverty in Mexico by a man who befriended her with sweets and a story. She spent four years being forced to have sex 30 times a day. Her story isn't an unusual one for someone who has been or is being forced into sex trafficking. But it is one that brings exposure to the tricks of the enemy. Here, Karla shares in her own words her personal story from hell to healing, from victim to victory.

KARLA'S story in summary:

Karla says she was abused for as long as she can remember and felt rejected by her mother. "I came from a dysfunctional family. I was sexually abused and mistreated from the age of 5 by a relative,' she says. When she was twelve, she was targeted by a trafficker who lured her away using kind words and a fast car.

She says she was waiting for some friends near a subway station in Mexico City, when a little boy selling sweets came up to her, telling her somebody was sending her a piece of candy as a gift. Five minutes later, Karla says, an older man was talking to her, telling her that he was a used car salesman.

The initial awkwardness disappeared as soon as the man started telling her that he was also abused as a boy. He was also very affectionate and quite a gentleman, she says.

They exchanged phone numbers and when he called a week later, Karla says she got excited. He asked her to go on a trip to nearby Puebla with him and dazzled her by showing up driving a bright red Firebird Trans Am.

"When I saw the car I couldn't believe it. I was very impressed by such a big car. It was exciting for me. He asked me to get in the car to go places," she says.

It didn't take long for the man, who at 22 and was 10 years older than Karla, to convince her to leave with him, especially after Karla's mother didn't open the door one night when she came home a little too late.

"The following day I left with him. I lived with him for three months during which he treated me very well. He loved on me. He bought me clothes, gave me attention, bought me shoes, flowers, chocolates, everything was beautiful," Karla says.

But there were red flags everywhere also.

Karla says her boyfriend would leave her by herself for a week in their apartment. His cousins would show up with new girls every week. When she finally mustered the courage to ask what business they were in, he told her the truth. "We're pimps," he said.

A few days later he started telling her everything she had to do. The positions, how much she needed to charge, the things she had to do with the client and for how long. How she was to treat them and how she had to talk to them so that they would give me more money," Karla says.

It was the beginning of four years of hell. The first time she was forced to work as a prostitute she was taken to Guadalajara, one of Mexico's largest cities.

She started at 10 a.m. and finished at midnight. They were in Guadalajara for a week. Do the math. Twenty per day for a week. Some men would laugh at her because I was crying. She had to close her eyes so that she wouldn't see what they were doing to her, so that she wouldn't feel anything," Karla says.

There would be several other cities. She would be sent to brothels, roadside motels, streets known for prostitution and even homes. There were no holidays or days off, and after the first few days, she was made to see at least 30 customers a day, seven days a week. Karla tells how she was attacked by her trafficker after a john gave her a hickey. He started beating her with a chain all over her body. He punched her with his fists, he kicked her, pulled her hair, spit at her in the face and that day was when he also burned her with the iron. She told him she wanted to leave and he was accusing her of falling in love with a customer. He told me her she liked being a whore.

One day, when she was working in Mexico, at a hotel known for prostitution, police showed up. They kicked out of all of the customers, Karla says, and shut down the hotel. She thought it was her lucky day -- a police operation to rescue her and the other girls. Her relief quickly turned to horror when the officers, about 30 she says, took the girls to several rooms and started shooting video of them in compromising positions. The girls were told the videos would be sent to their families if they didn't do everything they' re told.

She thought they were disgusting. They knew the girls were minors. they were not even developed. They had sad faces. There were girls who were only 10 years old. There were girls who were crying. They told the officers they were minors and nobody paid attention," Karla says. She was 13 years old at the time.

In her nightmare world even a pregnancy was cause for horror not joy. Karla gave birth at 15 to a girl -- a baby fathered by the pimp who would use the daughter to tighten the noose around her neck: if she didn't fulfill his every wish, he would either harm or kill the baby. He took the baby away from her a month after the baby was born, and she was not allowed to see her again until the girl was more than a year old.

Karla Jacinto was finally rescued in 2008 during an anti-trafficking operation in Mexico City. Her ordeal lasted four very long and tormenting years. She was still a minor, only 16, when it ended -- but she has endured a lifetime of horror that will stay with her as long as she lives.

Determination and courage came into Karla's life. She had a story to tell and she had been given an audience to share it with. As she spoke with the reporter, she looked him straight into his eyes. Her voice cracking slightly, as she tells him the number she wanted him to remember -- 43,200.

By her own estimate, 43,200 is the number of times she was raped after falling into the hands of human traffickers. She says up to 30 men a day, seven days a week, for the best part of four years -- 43,200.

Karla's story highlights the brutal realities of human trafficking in Mexico and the United States, an underworld that has destroyed the lives of tens of thousands of young girls and boys. Human trafficking has become a trade so lucrative and prevalent, that it knows no borders and links towns in central Mexico with cities like Atlanta, Los Angeles and New York.

U.S. and Mexican officials both point to a town in central Mexico that for years has been a major source of human trafficking rings and a place where victims are taken before being eventually forced into prostitution.

Even though it has a population of about 13,000 it has an oversized reputation when it comes to prostitution and pimping. Says Susan Coppedge, who is now the U.S. State Department's Ambassador at Large to Combat Human trafficking. She previously worked at the U.S. Attorney's office in Atlanta.

"That's what the town does. That is their industry," Coppedge says. "And yet in smaller, rural communities the young girls don't have any idea that this is what the town's reputation is. So they are not suspicious of the men who come from there. They think they have got a great future with this person. They think they are loved and it is the same story of recruitment every time."

CNN independently verified portions of Karla's story. We have spoken with United Against Human Trafficking group she was referred to after being rescued and to senior officials at Road to Home, a shelter where Karla lived for one year after her rescue. Due to the clandestine nature of the human trafficking business, corroborating everything Karla told us is not possible.

Karla is now 23 years old. She has become an outspoken advocate against human trafficking, and telling her story at conferences and public events.

She told her story to Pope Francis in July at the Vatican. She also told the U.S. Congress in May. Her testimony was used as evidence in support for H.R. 515 or Megan's Law that mandates U.S. authorities share information pertaining to American child sex offenders when these convicts attempt to travel abroad.

Her message is that human trafficking and forced prostitution still happens and is a growing problem in our world. Karla says: "These minors are being abducted, lured, and yanked away from their families. Don't just listen to me. You need to learn about what happened to me and take the blindfold off your eyes."

Doing nothing, she says, puts countless girls at risk of being trafficked for years and raped tens of thousands of times, just like she was.

How horrible to have been forced to live in such a condition. Karla was looking for love only to find herself in an abusive relationship. The sad thing in this story is that her own mother abused her mentally and physically.

Everyone won't have the ear of Congress or the Pope; but what you will gain will be a greater reward than the approval of man when you learn to walk in forgiveness.

LAURA'S STORY

Laura is a young girl who was a prostitute from a very young age. She had no self-value. She tells of her relationship with a man, Robert. Who sexually, mentally and physically abused her to the point where she thought she was going to die. He literally attempted to kill her. Laura found her value and worth by standing up before everyone, especially her abuser, and telling her story.

I was 17 around the time I met 'Robert.' It started off with me and my friend meeting him for social purposes. It just went on for about nine months and we were living in different hotels the entire time. I don't even remember how many men there were. I was a runaway and wasn't living anywhere stable, so since I was underage most of the time, I sort of needed him in order to get hotels and move around.

I had already been a prostitute since I was 15. I think I just didn't even know what was right or wrong and how I should be treated. Towards the end, he held me against my will in a hostage situation. Forced me to prostitute, took all the money and just beat me severely. The last time I saw him, he was just beating me until he was absolutely tired. I was covered in bruises and my face was completely disfigured. It's causing me issues with my back to this day because of the way he was beating me and torturing me. That was probably the worst. There was a client in the room and he was having an issue with something I couldn't do because I was all beat up. I didn't want to do it anymore. I didn't want to do anything. He wanted the money back. When Robert and he were talking I ran out of the room and somehow was able to run faster than him.

I didn't tell anyone. I kept it to myself until I got a call from the FBI that he'd been arrested for something else and asked would I talk. Having to go face everything and realize how serious the abusive treatment and forced prostitution was. For the longest time I didn't even think it was that serious. At the trial, it felt empowering to look at him the entire time. I'm sure it drove him crazy. He can never touch me but he had to look at me and listen and it made me feel good.

I had to learn that if I don't at least have some kind of love and value for myself, no one ever will. My advice to other girls would be to let people help you. It's not your fault and that you didn't deserve it. It's OK to be hurt about it because a lot of people will act like it never happened, because that's what I was going to do too. [..]

Take Laura's advice and let others help you. You are not alone! You are valuable and precious to God. There is a real and safe love to be had. You first got to trust God and let Him in to renew your thinking. Believing that He is your healer and redeemer and that His plan for you is real. Laura did and so can you.

APRIL'S STORY

> *I was 15 at the time and was a runaway. 'Tom' wanted to be a pimp. So I would be in his room, in his apartment and he would not let me go out for anything. He tried to intimidate me by threatening to beat me up if I tried to leave. I was scared of him so I wouldn't leave. He would drop me off at a hotel while he went to work.*
>
> *It lasted from March until June or July. Sometimes it would be every day. Sometimes he would say, "not today, but tomorrow." Out of the week, maybe 4-5 times a week, I was with different men. I just felt like that it was my fault. I deserved it and nobody would ever believe me or try to help me. So I just let them control how I thought about myself. They were always verbally abusive and putting me down. It got to the point that I actually started believing it.*
>
> *Just by letting someone control your freedom and take over just what you say or do is the definition of slavery to me. I couldn't leave the room. It was like 'wow, I'm letting someone make me feel so scared all the time.*
>
> *I never called the police because I felt it was my fault because I felt like I had to stay. One day the FBI ended up coming to my house and contacted me because my name came up in their investigation. During this investigation is when I felt like I had to tell my story to ensure my freedom. I was free and empowered by telling it all. I am now free from bondage and slavery of any kind.[...]*

These stories are just examples of what many girls and women have encountered, and perhaps your story is similar. Despite all you have been through, it's important to remember you have self-worth.

Each one of these young ladies made a decision to stand up for themselves against the worst human condition imaginable. Every life story that has been shared throughout this book has been given to show you that you can live past your hurt, pain, and shame. You can be completely freed from its power. You can celebrate knowing you survived! You are stronger now than before. Find the lessons in your story and draw strength and confidence from it. You may be reading these words of God's faithfulness in salvation and transformation and find yourself on the outside looking in. Or perhaps the religious road you've been on it before and you don't feel much like you have or deserves this grace of God you are reading about here. Don't allow the enemy to keep you in doubt and disbelief. I have given you much evidence that God is real and His is Word is truth for you. Maybe you've tasted and seen the grace of God and today is your new beginning to walk in that grace, each and every day. An invitation and welcome have been offered to you to come as broken, hopeless, and burdened, and find peace for your soul. In Matthew 11:28 (NLT) Jesus says, Come to Me, all you who are weary and carry heavy burdens, and I will give you rest. The Gospel – the good news of Jesus Christ – is simply this: in Christ Jesus you have reached the end to earning His favor, the end to self-reliance, the end to slavery to sin, the end to condemnation (guilt and shame), the end to being to be good enough. You are now living a new beginning in surrender and letting go of every sin and bondage, a new beginning in forgiveness (especially forgiving yourself), a new beginning in holiness (Christ led), a new beginning in freedom, a new beginning in loving Christ and much more!

Celebrate now! Here's to your new beginning!

CONCLUSION

A while ago, I shared my unedited version of this book with a very close friend of mine. She told me that when she started reading my introduction, she had to stop reading it.

"You write like you're angry," she said. To her, it was as if I went back to the room where the molestation happened, and it was too real for her. At first, offense tried to creep up in my heart and plant a seed of division there. I felt she was rejecting me and my writing. (Remember, rejection was one of my deep-seated fears.) The enemy wanted me to get mad and cut off my relationship with my girl. But I knew she loved me, and I didn't want to lose a trusting sister because of my issues.

But she was right about one thing, I am angry against an enemy whose aim was to take me out of the game of life. I am angry because this same enemy wants to take you out!

Perhaps you feel the same way. If so, it's okay that you are angry about what happened or is happening to you. I encourage you not to use your experience as an excuse to stay angry, frustrated, helpless, or hopeless. Such toxicity can cause you to sin against yourself or others. The Bible points this out in Ephesians 4:26-27: "In your anger do not sin": Do not let the sun go down while you are still angry, and do not give the devil a foothold." It's not okay to stay broken and abused when you now know how to get better. After hearing my friend's critiques, I realized this book isn't for everyone and that's okay. It was written to you and for you; a person who has been hurt, abused, battered, and mistreated. The enemy does not want you to believe the truths written here. He does not want you to find healing and hope for your future. His plan is to only steal, kill, and destroy your life (John 10:10). He doesn't want you to know that the abuse was not your fault. He wants you to live in shame and condemnation so that you aren't effective in your gifts and calling. Evil is just that, evil. Many of us cannot comprehend why (evil) people do what they do. But we must be willing to forgive our past and the evil done to us so we can move forward. We are called to love our enemies, and pray for those who persecute you. (Matthew 5:44 NIV). This <u>is a</u> commandment from God, and one that comes with rewards. The Bible teaches us that we must be aware of the tricks and traps of the enemy. The devil prowls around like a roaring lion, looking for ways to devour you (1 Peter 5:8). But you have the power to stop him from gaining access in your life. The more you draw closer to God, the more you will be able to resist the devil.

    It took some <u>time for me to</u> trust <u>God's</u> love and plan for my life the way I do today. But I did so by making bold declarations over my life each day:

- Today, I declare I chose not to give another day to the devil's control.
- Today, I declare my life is in Christ.
- Today, I live for Him and Him alone.
- Today, I am sold out to His commands.
- Today, I released my all to Him.

    I am not <u>confused</u> to <u>who I am</u> and <u>where I am going.</u> I know <u>that</u> it was <u>by the grace of God</u> that <u>I am</u> alive. <u>I am</u> thankful every day <u>for</u> His goodness in my life. I could have been physically dead or a broken woman barely existing. But God's hand was upon me for good! He had so much more for me to do, and He has so much more for you to accomplish.

    You, too, can, add I encourage you to make bold statements about your life. Here are a few declarations based on the passages in Ephesians 1-6:

1. I am Chosen.
2. I am Saved.
3. I am Free.

4. I am a New Creation.
5. I am Dearly Loved.
6. I am Fully Equipped.

You are rising up from the pit and ashes of hell. Embrace the new you, for you are beautifully and wonderfully created.

Before we conclude this book, let's look at the lessons from each strategy:

1. Always remember that it's not your fault! Only you can tell the story of your past. Only you can write your story of your new beginning.
2. Always remember to rip off the mask! No more pretending. The Mask has been ripped off and permanently removed. Believe you will no longer live a life full of fear and doubt. Say, "Here I am, take it or leave it. I will no longer hide because of the shameful things someone else did to me or I did to myself. I am free! I am loved, precious, and wanted!"
3. Always remember to never be afraid to expose the predator! The Predator has many faces and names. You are no longer responsible for its actions. You can confront it and call it by name. It's time to tell someone. You are not alone! Your power comes in your telling.
4. Always remember to stop the blame game! You will never get an apology from the abuser or for the abuse. You can never be paid enough for your pain, so let it go and forgive. By forgiving, you have chosen to move beyond the past towards your new future. By forgiving you have taken back your power and control.
5. Always remember to never live in denial. Instead, make the decision to live! By now, you have made what you feel is the right decision for your life. Live your life without excuses.
6. And finally, always remember to celebrate your now! You made it through the pain and abuse. You are alive today. No one can move you out of this freedom

you have in Christ Jesus. It's time to celebrate the good in your life and forget the things that have damaged you in your old life.

The great thing about all the promises in this book is that they are not Betty's promises. They are God's Awesome Promises for you. As I stated earlier in this book, God gave me the ministry of God's Awesome Promises (G.A.P.MIN) in the mid to late 90s. I believe God will use GAPMIN to change lives across the nation and around the world.

At GAPMIN, our vision is to be the global ministry in restoring wholeness to girls and women who are victims of sexual, mental, and physical abuse. We fulfill our vision by offering group and one-on-one counseling/coaching using our S.T.O.P. (Stand, Take, Own & Protect) Program. Which empowers, equips, and restores girls and women back to God's original purpose He has for them.

We use six strategies over twelve weeks that are written within this program. We personalize the steps based on individual or group needs.

We are confident that when you are provided a safe place to share their stories, you will be encouraged and empowered to embrace all the promises God has for you. I pray this book brings you as much healing as it did for me in writing it. Be blessed.

ABOUT GOD'S AWESOME PROMISES MINISTRIES (G.A.P.MIN)

FOR MORE INFORMATION ON GOD'S AWESOME PROMISES MINISTRY CONTACT US AT GAPMINISTRIES@YAHOO.COM. VISION: GAP IS THE GLOBAL MINISTRY IN RESTORING WHOLENESS TO GIRLS AND WOMEN WHO ARE VICTIMS OF SEXUAL, MENTAL, AND PHYSICAL ABUSE. MISSION: WE FULFILL OUR VISION BY OFFERING GROUP AND INDIVIDUAL COACHING USING OUR S.T.O.P. PROGRAM, WHICH EMPOWERS, EQUIPS, AND RESTORES GIRLS AND WOMEN BACK TO GOD'S ORIGINAL PURPOSE HE HAS FOR THEM. ~'FOR I KNOW THE PLANS AND THOUGHTS THAT I HAVE FOR YOU', SAYS THE LORD, 'PLANS FOR PEACE AND WELL-BEING AND NOT FOR DISASTER TO GIVE YOU A FUTURE AND A HOPE. JEREMIAH 29:11 AMP

SHARE YOUR STORY

ABOUT THE AUTHOR

BETTY SHORT-SAMS lives in Elk Grove, California with her husband, Clifton, of over 34 years. She is the mother of one son, Darnell, and is a loving mother in love to her daughter in love, Sonia. She is Gammie to her five grandchildren. She retired from law enforcement after 30 years of service. She is a veteran of the United States Navy, where she served proudly. She is Founder and CEO of God's Awesome Promises Ministries, GAPMIN, a ministry used by God in restoring wholeness to girls and women who are victims of sexual, mental, and physical abuse. She is a passionate woman of God who believes in speaking God's word of life and His truth in the lives of all who He gives her opportunity to. Being empowered by the Spirit of God she accomplishes this through speaking and teaching engagements. By using her Christian counselor and life experiences she is well equipped by God to counsel and coach individuals and groups to be themselves empowered, equipped and restored. Betty believes strongly in being transparent about her abuse and struggles. As you read in this book you will understand that through her struggles God delivered her from a life spent in shame, guilt and pain. Her goal in writing this book is to let all who read know that there is a God who saves, and His name is Jesus!

Made in the USA
San Bernardino, CA
23 August 2019